ON POETRY, CULTURE,
AND DEMOCRACY

On Poetry, Culture, and Democracy

ROBERT PINSKY

WITH A NEW PREFACE BY THE AUTHOR

PRINCETON UNIVERSITY PRESS

PRINCETON & OXFORD

The Situation of Poetry was first published by Princeton University Press as part of the series Princeton Essays in Literature. *Democracy, Culture and the Voice of Poetry* was first published by Princeton University Press as part of The University Center for Human Values Series.

Published by Princeton University Press
41 William Street, Princeton, New Jersey 08540
99 Banbury Road, Oxford OX2 6JX
press.princeton.edu

GPSR Authorized Representative: Easy Access System Europe - Mustamäe tee 50, 10621 Tallinn, Estonia, gpsr.requests@easproject.com

All Rights Reserved

   ISBN (pbk.) 9780691278254
   ISBN (epub) 9780691290041
   ISBN (PDF) 9780691278261

Library of Congress Control Number: 2025948828

British Library Cataloging-in-Publication Data is available

Editorial: Erik Beranek
Production Editorial: Theresa Liu
Jacket/Cover Design: Chris Ferrante
Production: Lauren Reese
Publicity: Natalie Zander

Cover image: *On the Boardwalk from Bert's Place, Seaside Heights, N.J.,* ca. 1930–1945. Tichnor Brothers Collection. Boston Public Library, Arts Department. Courtesy of Digital Commonwealth.

This book has been composed in Arno

Printed in the United States of America

10 9 8 7 6 5 4 3 2 1

CONTENTS

PREFACE

THE TWO BOOKS collected here, *The Situation of Poetry* and *Democracy, Culture and the Voice of Poetry*, were published, respectively, in 1976 and 2002—twenty-five years apart, and the more recent one twenty-five years ago.

In the first, a judgmental young poet implies his agenda; in the other, an older one has been assigned to deliver the Tanner Lectures in Human Values at Princeton University . . . and he implies his agenda. Both books are animated by the idea that poetry is a bodily art. Its medium is breath: each reader's actual or imagined voice, and not necessarily the voice of the poet or any other performer.

Democracy, too, has involved a human-scale voice, the dignity of the individual person, with an emphasis on spoken language: an ancient tradition so strong that the 1939 movie *Mr. Smith Goes to Washington* sentimentalizes the filibuster, with its enduring appeal like the institution of the town hall. Among the speechwriter/rhetors of Athens, the innovator Isocrates was celebrated for tailoring each speech to the particular, individual speaker who hired him. The art of writing in a plain style that resembles conversational or personal speech has been expressed in terms with cultural or even political implications: "ordinary language," language "that dogs and cats can understand," "plain talk," "street language"—or most explicitly, the scholarly word "*demotic*" echoing, by way of etymology and *demos*, the paramount importance of eloquence in the short-lived Athenian democracy and its long aftermath.

Now, in 2026, long after writing these two books, I reconsider them in what feels like a time of cultural debasement or cynicism, a turning not only against works of art I value, but even against the American ideal of secular, public education that formed my parents and me. Do these books offer any counter-force?

Or is that sense of decay I feel just a classic sign of old age? Looking for historical guidance, I wince as I read again the Tanner Lecture passage where I quote the aristocratic 19th-century visitor Alexis de Tocqueville:

> Nothing conceivable is so petty, so insipid, so crowded with paltry interests—in one word, so anti-poetic—as the life of a man in the United States.

I feel again the urgency of tempering that sentence by quoting de Tocqueville's additional, qualifying statement, where he says that in our country, "The principle of equality does not, then, destroy all the subjects of poetry: it renders them less numerous, but more vast."

My earliest personal experiences of poetry as an art reinforces for me the truth of that insight. A demotic or democratic national poetry, possibly lacking the richness of ancient myths and stories, might confront subjects that are vast because they are fundamental.

But the way toward those subjects, access to them, must be sensuous, by which I mean vocal. As a personal example, certain lines by Emily Dickinson came into me, when and where I can't remember, through the physical experience of saying them. These verses gave me a formative experience of poetry's peculiar combination of bodily with intellectual pleasure. Essential to that combination is a moment, or the momentum, of mind anticipating and formulating speech, preparing for the power of breath, the vowels shaped by an artful, bodily, you might even say athletic deployment of consonants and vowels:

> Further in Summer than the Birds
> Pathetic from the Grass
> A minor Nation celebrates
> Its unobtrusive Mass,

I found myself wondering, intensely, what it might feel like if you needed to say these exact words. Thinking that way, saying the words over to yourself, maybe just muttering them, or saying them not actually but in your mind's ear, and imagining them, even feeling them, as something you *needed to say*—the poet possesses your voice. Not to exaggerate—not necessarily possessing your understanding or your feelings—but yes, your voice. The lines had something that made me want them, to say them in my mind's voice, and maybe even out loud, as well.

Without my needing to try, Dickinson's lines entered my memory. In that sense, I possessed them. But more profoundly, the lines possessed me, partly through their physical, vocal grace and penetration, but also by the ways they are, in their invocation of that "unobtrusive Mass" both historical and a-historical—or maybe more accurately "anti-historical"?

So early in my life was my encounter with this poem, I may not have known that "Mass" is more Catholic than Protestant.

I was probably too young, also, to appreciate the cultural overtones of "minor." The poem undermines or disclaims those overtones, and the religious connotations of its terms, at least as much as it invokes them. Not until years later did I register that "further in summer" places the emergence of insects much later in the season than "the Birds." That naturalist's accuracy contrasts with the possibly comic or skeptical quality of the references.

The poet's complicated, half-alienated devotion to vast religious concerns was different from my uninformed first encounter with the poem. But a beginning of knowledge, in this illuminated beginning of Emily Dickinson's poem, came into my memory, near the core, thanks to a part of my brain related to speech. Whatever happens in the neurological process of saying something became enlisted, by the syntactical melody of these lines, into the process of understanding. The comprehension of a vast subject—something about the sacred and the ordinary, about intuition and ordinance—was vocal.

That experience underlies an assumption in these books. The primary medium for a poem is bodily: the vocal faculty of any engaged reader. That individual-scale, vocal medium, the extreme opposite of "mass media," gives the art of poetry a unique significance in American culture and society.

That viewpoint still guides my thinking about the art of poetry and poetry's place in the world, social and cultural. Central to the more recent of these two books *Democracy, Culture and the Voice of Poetry*, I hope that same viewpoint implicitly guides the most "inside-baseball" passages of *The Situation of Poetry*, even when it sizes up new books of the late 1970s. The worldly situation of poetry, that can seem small by common measures, gains immense importance from the individual, human scale of one voice at a time. In any particular example, poetry may be great or dopey, large or small, wise or stupid. But inherently, by its vocal nature, the art is as grand as its respect for the dignity of the individual. Also, the art of poetry in any instance can be as limited, petty or insipid as the understanding of any reader, and even of the greatest poets.

The scope of poetry's voice can expand infinitely beyond the epic, or it can concentrate beyond the microscopic. About the "minor nation" and its "unobtrusive Mass" Dickinson's poem goes on to say:

> No Ordinance be seen
> So gradual the Grace
> A pensive Custom it becomes
> Enlarging Loneliness.

Loneliness, without explicit or dramatic flourishes, in a singular, peculiar ritual intensifies to become not only more itself— more lonely—but also *enlarged*: vast beyond any institutional "Ordinance," and beyond the prescribed range of the habitual, the autocratic machinery of oppression, the petty rules of bureaucracy, or the ordinances of pedantry.

In 1976, when *The Situation of Poetry* was published, the president of the United States was Gerald Ford, who had pardoned his criminal predecessor, Richard Nixon. In 2002, when *Democracy, Culture and the Voice of Poetry* was published, the newly elected president was George W. Bush, who would respond to the terrorist attacks of September 11, 2001 by undertaking the military invasion of Afghanistan and then of Iraq.

Historical realities as manifold as these find their way into a life, and into poetry, in a multitude of ways. Readers who expect these two books to discourse about the Ford and Bush administrations, Nixon and Iraq, will be as disappointed as readers who might assume that the books will deal directly with categories such as the beats, the confessionals, the New York school, or with the poets laureate and winners of prizes in 1976 or 2002. In another limitation, also absent are the influential critics of the decades when these books appeared.

I try to come at important things in my own way. Like the high school student quoted on page 283, reflecting on the Khmer Rouge, relating her family's history and cultures to her own concerns, and to a poem by Langston Hughes, I take an approach that is inclusive and personal, based on the basic human value of speech, in the spirit of art.

I have lived in some bewilderment, with some effort to understand, through both kinds of history that I have cited, national and poetic, as well as social and political and cultural. I am still trying to feel my own limited way through those kinds of history, as best as I can. I hope that in one idiosyncratic, biased, tentative or audacious way or another, however indirectly, these two books deal with all of the above.

ON POETRY, CULTURE,
AND DEMOCRACY

The Situation of Poetry

CONTEMPORARY POETRY

AND ITS TRADITIONS

(1976)

To the Memory of
B. E.
and of
A. Y. W.

PREFACE

This is not a survey, nor a selection of the best or most promising work being done. Rather, I try to explore principles: some of the problems and opportunities of this current moment in poetry. Those problems and opportunities may be defined by considering what part the poetry of the past, especially the poetry of the immediate past, seems to play in the mind of one who is about to read or to write a poem.

The traditions meant by my subtitle are modernist and, beyond that, Romantic. I have in mind something a little like the relation between the later seventeenth-century English poets and the earlier ones. Not that poets now writing are doomed to be at best mere Wallers and Lovelaces compared to the Donnes and Jonsons of fifty years ago; rather, theory and practice in an art may at some times change radically and swiftly or, at other times, at a kind of historical minimum pace.

Such historical changes in the way poets write, and in ideas about poetry, interest me more than the alleged "influence" of one writer upon another. Indeed, "influence" is a problematic concept, in that it assumes a simple causality where such causality can rarely, if ever, be demonstrated. The better the writing, the more likely it is that "affinity" will be a more useful word. The complex idea of causal "influence," as distinct from the older and simpler idea of imitation or emulation, is itself a continuing idea, or tradition.

In fact, the idea of influence, insofar as it emphasizes the irresistible force of one personality upon another, is a Romantic tradition, implying that poetry expresses unique internal forces rather than imitating an objective world by technical means that may be shared. For me, the neutral terms "affinity" and "tradition" offer ways to discuss how a poet may have been affected by other poets: by unlikely combinations of poets, by minor poets, by an idiosyncratic personal favorite, or even by a poet one does not much respect. The poet may carve out a conscious or unconscious model combining the Anglo-Saxon poem *Deor*, a phrase from a bad translation of Vergil he once read, and a trick of Campion's. For the most part, such webs are invisible and undiscussable.

When the network of reference and reliance in relation to the past is visible, and is discussable, and is in fact part of the poem's technique—a technique that openly or tacitly depends upon the reader sharing the same experience of past writing—then the term "tradition" applies. This book is an essay about the current state of the modernist tradition. In it, I assume that the force of a tradition is normally felt through an intricate, shifting constellation of poems, as through the air we breathe, and—with perhaps an exception or two—not through some single, necessarily major poet or poem.

"Contemporary" for present purposes will refer roughly to work appearing since, or not much before, 1959, when I first encountered the delights and wisdoms of the art, as practiced by living poets. Roughly speaking, I begin with the safer ground of work by older writers and move toward younger generations as I go.

ACKNOWLEDGMENTS

Parts of the following chapters and sections of this book have been published previously, in considerably different form:

Chapter II, part IV in *Agenda* (Spring–Summer 1972).

Chapter IV, part II in *Parnassus* (Summer 1975).

Chapter IV, part III in *The Rarer Action: Essays in Honor of Francis Fergusson*, ed. Cheuse and Koffler (Rutgers University Press, 1970).

Chapter V, part IV in *Poetry* (January 1974).

I am grateful to the editors of these journals, and of *The Rarer Action*, for permission to use this material.

For their valuable advice and encouragement, I am indebted to Pamela Ezequelle, John Peck, and Ellen Pinsky—among others. Thanks are due to the National Endowment for the Humanities and to Wellesley College, for their support.

I. Introduction

I. "Modern" and "Contemporary"

Modern poetry was created by writers born about a hundred years ago. The premises of their work included a mistrust of abstraction and statement, a desire to escape the blatantly conventional aspects of form, and an ambition to grasp the fluid, absolutely particular life of the physical world by using the static, general medium of language. Those premises are paradoxical, or at the least peculiar, in themselves. Moreover, the brilliant stylistic inventions associated with the premises—notably the techniques of "imagism," which convey the powerful illusion that a poet presents, rather than tells about, a sensory experience—are also peculiar as techniques.

Or, they once seemed peculiar. These special, perhaps even tormented premises and ways of writing have become a tradition: a climate of implicit expectation and tacit knowledge. As such a tradition remains alive, it changes and grows, and much of the growth consists of extending principles further in their logical directions. As a general example, to be filled in later,[1] consider those contemporary poems that tend, pretty distinctly as such matters go, toward coolness: the aspect of modernism that effaces or holds back the warmth of authorial commitment to feeling or idea, in favor of a surface cool under the reader's initial touch.

A previous generation sometimes sought such coolness of surface through concentration on objective images. But the indirect, imagistic manner of, say, Williams's "Spring and All" or Stevens's "The World as Meditation" can seem explicit, moralizing, rhetorical compared to the amused remoteness of, say, James Tate's "Blue Booby" or Jim Harrison's "Trader."[2] For many contemporary poets, the effective practice seems to be based upon a particular kind of voice: enigmatic, slangy, fey, tough, idiosyncratic, darting between the plain and the daffy with a mock-naive, teenage sort of detachment. That detachment, a knowing, ironic superiority to parts of one's own mind and experience—the "cool" of high school in the early sixties or late fifties—defines the manner for me better than reference to surrealism or location in California or New York. To some extent, the poems of Stevens, Williams, and other modernists have supplied this later manner with a starting point, an aesthetic equivalent or crystallizing form. It seems worthwhile to investigate the strength and nature of that continuity.

My thesis in this book is that we learn many of our attitudes toward language and reality from the past, and that it takes considerable effort by a poet either to understand and apply those attitudes, for his own purposes, or to abandon them. The alternative to such effort may be to lapse into mere mannerism or received ideas. All of this seems to be particularly true because we have a body of great poetry in our recent past. That poetry, modern poetry, the formidable work done by Crane, Eliot, Frost, Pound, Stevens, Williams, Yeats, and others, has been dealt with in such penetrating detail that we have many alternative, illuminating ways to describe it.[3] Poetic modernism, often a self-defining, introspective art to start with, still exerts all the momentum and attraction of a successful revolution; academically, modernism has already become one of the most skillfully studied, the most ingeniously explained, of the historical periods of poetry in English. And while the poetry of that period recedes into the historical, it remains fairly widely read, quoted, and admired, and not only by professional scholars.

But while modern poetry constitutes a distinct and perhaps even a massive entity, especially at American universities, little of value has been done to show how, or whether, modern poetry operates as a heritage, let alone as a tradition, for contemporary poetry. Modern poetry often expressed or implied certain persistent ambitions, ambitions that have to do with giving the poem some of the status of an object or phenomenon, rather than a statement. Though one cannot apply the idea in Procrustean fashion to all contemporary poems, a surprisingly wide range of work does seem to be illuminated by considering such inherited motives, and the techniques associated with them.

Moreover, those inherited motives involve a conflict, potentially severe, between the poet's medium and, on the other hand, his convictions about reality and art. His medium ties the poet to words, which are conventional referents, and to sentences, which are—even when fragmented—conventional arrangements. And verse by definition implies recurrence, if only a recurrence to the left-hand margin. Pound[4] tells us to go in fear of abstractions, but recurrence is an abstract form, and every word is an abstraction or category, not a particular: "foot" is no more concrete than "trepidation" or "cosine," and "large foot" or "Robert's large foot" merely add categories.

The poet's medium, then, is abstract, more or less discursive, and in some senses conventional. But his convictions about reality and art are likely to be pervaded by the idea that reality inheres in particulars, not abstractions; in experience, not in discourse or convention. Experience may well seem fluid and instantaneous, but language is sequential and, once uttered, relatively fixed. These are the broad, cold outlines of a conflict that inspired the dazzling solutions and accomplishments of modernism, an extraordinary, manifold transformation of poetry in English. The conflict and the accomplishments remain, and have their relevance to most of the work, good and bad, in current numbers of *Poetry* magazine or in new volumes of poetry.

Finally, it is no mere hedge to add that the exceptions are of interest partly because they *are* exceptions; and that, having inherited a tradition, one may deal with it by eschewing it or reacting against it. Some conventions operate most clearly when they are violated or discarded, like the proscenium arch, the boundary line in a game, the omniscient narrator, a mating custom, a given poetic diction. For instance, the blank verse of Keats, Landor, and Wordsworth will offer more delight and wisdom to the reader who understands that the poet has cultivated an avoidance of the mere Miltonism that plagued the eighteenth century. (In the same way, one can better perceive the controlled lushness of diction and line in the blank verse of Wallace Stevens in the light of his freedom from Victorian

Keatsism.) The avoided possibility is not simply negative, but also a principle the artist exploits, knowingly attaining new virtues impossible without it, impossible perhaps to comprehend without it. Nor did the nineteenth-century poets I have named need to forget all that they learned from Milton, in order not to Miltonize.

There are more direct, specific ways to support the contention that contemporary poetry is by and large traditional. In beginning to take up the job of such proof, and the job of exemplifying the term "tradition," I will try to illustrate the idea first in the relatively obvious case of unsuccessful work; then, in the more elusive, more interesting relationship between a successful poem and its traditional element. In the first instance, the examples involve the traditional nature of a specific device, or bit of style; in the second, a concept.

II. Examples

I will start where I hope not to end, with the borrowing of attitudes and mannerisms (often trivial) indicated by the expression "derivative." It is easy—and ultimately not enough, however instructive—to find descendants of Pound's testy ellipsis, or his use of foreign words like "polis" for monumental concepts; Crane's combination of high language with physically high visual perspective in lyrical-ironic city scenes; Eliot's choral, sinister adaptations of baby talk, slang, noises; Yeats's use of stylized, rather pre-Raphaelite physical gestures as poetic shorthand for emotions, as in "rocked and sobbed," "danced and cried out," etc.; or Williams's charmingly informal addresses to his wife, mother, neighbors. While such instances prove only the most mechanical aspect of a tradition, the stubbornly recurrent ones may reveal matters of deeper significance.

That is, mere similarity with the past does not necessarily indicate a living relationship with it; the outer husk may persist without the spirit, or only the spirit of ornament. Yet the nature of the tradition may show itself in those ornaments, however hollow, which do persist; for instance, the egregiously "fresh" descriptive similitude (like a comic's one-line gag) when the device means essentially that the writer has the status of a poet: inventive, observant, unpredictable.

This characteristic figure can serve as an emblem for one important, continuing strain in the style of modernist poetry. At one of its sources, in Wallace Stevens's pineapple that is

> the coconut and cockerel in one

or in Marianne Moore's fir trees

> each with an emerald turkey-foot at the top

attention to the context will show that the dandyism is virtually always not naive, but ironic. Stevens or Moore may nod, and this irony itself may become mechanical and second-rate—but it is there, a sort of stylistic diffident cough, a self-effacing exaggeration of gesture. By means of it, the poet indicates both his wish to vanish in favor of the object, and his inability to do so as totally as the descriptive power of the same, oddball image or analogy promises.

As Hugh Kenner says of Moore, an essential aim is:

> ... to avoid implying that a cat or a fish has never really been looked at before.[5]

Stevens often builds overripe alliteration and assonance in a similar spirit; the figures of sound embody an elegantly apologetic derision, directed at the regrettable intrusion into a poem of the poet's own imagination, foppish and cavorting. This alliterative mode or trick of Stevens's seems essentially his own, with no host of descendants comparable to the million gems of contemporary "description" or "impressionism" that are essentially exhibitionist in motive.

By "exhibitionist" I mean that the aggressive yoking of unlike things can sometimes amount to little more than showing off. Unlike Moore or Stevens the poet does try, precisely, to imply that a cat or a fish has never really been looked at before. A main contemporary form of the bardic, such writing ranges from the enigmatically poetical, as in the solemn poem called "Silence," which begins

> The fall has come, clear as the eyes of chickens[6]

to the ingenious entertainment or set piece, as in the poem or group of poems inviting the reader to look at the cardinal numbers through a poet's eye:

> 3 Shallow mitten for a two-fingered hand

> 4 Three-cornered hut
>   on one stilt. Sometimes built
>   so the roof gapes.[7]

These examples, especially the first, hold out an inherited mannerism without fully understanding it, so that it becomes a kind of gaud or badge establishing that the writer is a poet; the mannerism is like an ancestral tool whose function has been lost. The second example simply asks the reader to admire an acquired way of writing for its own sake, in the absence of a living subject; the fanciful or analogical manner is not reflected upon, but instead is limply accepted as though it had always been there, and therefore is interesting in itself, a part of life.

This is a negative sense of tradition: some hard-won, complex part of the historical inheritance is taken for granted; we forget that it *is* historical and full of meaning, and it is used for some trivial or base purpose: the spray-painted cobbler's bench, entwined with plastic foliage. Such examples illustrate the mastery and elaboration of a way of writing after the motives in life for that way of writing have become obscured. The presence of a powerful tradition, if it is ignored, can have that effect, leading us to expend force on self-regard at the expense of life, trivializing the ambitions of poetry. (Even the modest rights to life of a set piece can be trivialized, or not.)

Parenthetically, an important distinction can be made here: Moore or Stevens might imply that a fir tree or a pineapple has never been so well *described in words;* but that is to refer us as readers to the standard, ultimately, of our own experience of such fruits and trees. In contrast, the line quoted above tells us that our own experience of chickens and autumns is inferior or irrelevant. We are referred, ultimately, neither to the season nor to the fowl, but to what a deep imagination the poet has. This distinction underlies my use of "life" in the preceding paragraph, and what I understand Pound to mean by "the 'thing' whether subjective or objective."

This single unit of style—a certain kind of figure of speech, the egregious, clipped descriptive comparison—is not pre-

sented here as some kind of forbidden practice. Such a turn of
writing is neither good nor bad in itself, though it often may be
most clearly identifiable when least assimilated. The point is
that the device is significant and familiar; such prevalent man-
nerisms help to support the idea that a wide range of recent
poetic styles may share certain historical roots—both healthy
ones and otherwise.

The avoidance or converse of a convention also confirms its
force—expressed, for instance, as an irritation with the poten-
tial foppery of metaphor, a will perhaps to avoid it at all costs.
In effect, such purified or planed-down writing makes into prac-
tice, and into explicit declaration, what was implicit in the pen-
umbral, self-mocking overtones of Stevens. This style is the
symmetrical reverse of the lines just quoted, which preserve the
dandyism without the ironic reservations.

Robert Creeley, in this as in much else, shows a winning and
useful directness:

> Could write of fucking—
> rather its instant or the slow
> longing at times of its approach—
>
> how the young man desires,
> how, older, it is never known
> but, familiar, comes to be so.
>
> How your breasts, love,
> fall in a rhythm also familiar,
> neither tired nor so young they

> push forward. I hate the metaphors.
> I want you. I am still alone,
> but want you with me.[8]

The poet's resolve to avoid the dandyistic descriptive rhetoric of "the metaphors" appears here speaking with puritanical, nearly fanatical plainness. If the poem is not slack, it narrowly avoids slackness through the nervous pressure of that puritanism.

Consider another poem, called "Diction," in which Creeley laments

> The grand time when the words
> were fit for human allegation

Certainly, he has in mind more than the single kind of metaphor in question, aligning himself with the view, associated with Pound and Eliot, that language as a whole has been, or may become, debased. But more specifically, as the literary and even technical title, "Diction," suggests, part of the debasement originates with poets and "the metaphors." "The metaphors" exemplify what Creeley is at pains to avoid in the terrifically tentative, artificially "natural" language of the first Creeley poem quoted. This dogged, obsessive plainness works its way, in the second stanza

> how the young man desires,
> how, older, it is never known
> but, familiar, comes to be so

practically to the point of inarticulateness. And the descriptive third stanza avoids flashy rhetoric in favor of simple "human allegation" with such perceptible care that the effect is nearly fussy.

Creeley's poem seems to me quite different from the two fragments quoted earlier: worthy of taking seriously, and even as a pleasure. For instance, the sentence:

> How your breasts, love,
> fall in a rhythm also familiar,
> neither tired nor so young they
>
> push forward.

Without narcissism or pseudo-wit, the woman's body, moving, is associated companionably with the stirring of desire. The lines are credible, and therefore preserve the last stanza ("I am still alone . . .") from mere bathos. Though neither convincing as naturalistic speech nor persuasive as sharp physical description, these words about the human body achieve a patient, somewhat weary, sincerity. This quality of authenticity, rather like the moving gruffness of Barnabe Googe or George Gascoigne, is defined well enough by the word "allegation": not the thing itself, but words about the thing—and proud of it.

But if the fall that is "clear as the eyes of chickens" and the tediously clever "Cardinal Ideograms" put the poet between the poem and the reader, Creeley's language in this poem— so chastened that it seems to aspire toward some kind of non-language—does something similar. The puritan makes his reader too conscious of a matter as irrelevant as the dandy's "good imagination"; the poem is blocked by a sense of struggle, the writer trying desperately to follow his own directive to join art and life more sincerely than "the metaphors."

Moreover, what we get is less the struggle itself than its outward effects in a style of constant asides, conflicting tones whose relation to the subject is partly mysterious: without clear reason, the poem's tone is knowing, inhibited, fatigued, oddly self-conscious.

The "thing itself," the post-symbolist image, the whatever-we-call-it, does not appear in Creeley's poem as in the two earlier examples and the exaggerated style they can stand for: not, that is, as a once-powerful token, an uncomprehending savage ornament or an emblem of bardic rank; but it does appear as a kind of ghost. The modernist reservations about ornament, and indeed about words themselves, persist; while the image, the technique inspired by that mistrust, is itself spurned as one more form of ornamental verbiage. That is why the flat idiom of this poem seems worn down rather than sculpted. Its relation to a naively "imagistic" piece of writing recalls the saying that the ordinary man is ruined by the flesh lusting against the spirit, the scholar by the spirit lusting too much against the flesh. In neither case can the poem's relationship with a dominant past be made entirely successful.

I have tried to suggest the common roots of two varying and familiar contemporary styles, roots in modernist practices and issues. Perhaps every age has its plain style and its rhetorical style, but it is certainly not my purpose to divide all contemporary poetry into Fop and Puritan parties. Rather, the point is that in this the late modernist period both of those styles, and others, seem to base themselves upon some of the same grounds: prominently, a dissatisfaction with the abstract, discursive, and conventional nature of words as a medium for the particulars of experience.

That dissatisfaction may be expressed by pursuit of the physical image purified of statement, or in other instances by pursuit of an "allegation" purified of imagistic eloquence. In either case, the dissatisfaction is ultimately insoluble because of the nature of words and verses, but the great body of modern poetry demonstrates what a rich terrain of possibility the problem provides. The contemporary poet exploring that terrain will find himself in the presence of modernist terms and strategies.

II. Voices

I. Preliminary

In more successful and commandingly original work, matters of conception demand more attention than derived bits of style like the flash of descriptive analogy. Mere imitation is not the point. Rather, the work of the modern poets creates a source of unstated principles that are adapted or extended by the poet working in English as a natural part of his work at writing well, or the work of conceiving how to set up his poem's material. The recent past thus lives in the new poem, not in the way of neoclassical rules, but as certain ways of approaching the art that still, demonstrably, maintain their appeal in the minds of poets.

To show what I mean I will again rely on a very familiar idea. Recent years have shown (among many another current) an increasing turn away from the verbal complexity and elaborate "wit" associated with Eliot and some of the poets he admired; the same discernible tendency has also meant a drift away from the more bardic, declamatory qualities of Black Mountain, San

Francisco, other counter-Eliot writing of the fifties. In both cases, the new direction, cooler and quieter, suggests the paradoxical, essential, historically recurring poetic aim of sincerity. Yet, in the work of some well-known poets acknowledged as especially effective in the pursuit of personal feeling, intimate utterance, plain or "basic" material—say, John Berryman, Robert Lowell, Theodore Roethke—one can demonstrate, with only a little special choice of evidence, a shared, various tradition that might seem by definition "insincere": the so-called "mask" or "persona" of a million English Poetry classrooms.

The persistent strength of the idea of the persona appears in a negative proof, too: in the way that, for another group of poets, Frank O'Hara's growing importance as a model has to do partly with his systematic and conscious destruction of this dramatic element in the poem. (See O'Hara's mock-manifesto "Personism," in which the poem becomes a personal communication between two people.) More direct proof of the idea's continuing importance comes from its usefulness. It is hard to discuss intricately playful poems like John Ashbery's "Definition of Blue" without referring to "the speaker." Even Sylvia Plath, in poems like "Death & Co." and "The Bee Meeting," borrows some of the convention and manner of dramatic monologue in order to write about death and beyond (as did Emily Dickinson). And, an admirer of "The New Surrealism" suggests that the poet Bill Knott attains the neutral "anonymity" of the original surrealists by giving his own personality an exterior, posthumous, third-person identity, signing the poems "Bill Knott (1940–1966)."[1]

In short, the use of a borrowed voice or alter-identity, as speaker or central character partly distinct from the poet, constitutes one of the most widely noted, perhaps over-emphasized, critically chewed, and fundamental aspects of modernism. The concept has furnished the title and the theme for many a book of poems, and later for much good or indifferent critical prose. And "the speaker" as a method stands in clear logical relation to the modernist goal of moving the poem away from the abstraction of a statement, toward the being of an object. Unlike dramatic poems written before the nineteenth century, such poetry uses the dramatic mode as a way to keep intact a kind of silence or ambivalence; the gap between *res* and *verba* seems narrowed by making words into the particular experience of someone's speech.

But I have mentioned some recent poets: to varying degrees they seem to suspect the epic, the theological, the philosophical, the too obviously ambitious in any way, as potentially dry or inflated. With enormous differences, they share—and transform—the basic idea of using a speaker or protagonist who is not only dramatic, but somewhat eccentric, perhaps alien, as well. Though to a seventeenth-century reader that might seem a bizarre way of writing poems of personal feeling, the device is a common coin for poets and—equally so, which is the point—for their readers. We do not have to think about it; the convention (possibly too general to be called a "device") is so unremarkable to us, is accepted so easily, that among its variations the principle works more or less unseen, an anti-rhetorical kind of rhetoric. Such quiet workings of shared formal knowledge embody "tradition."

This particular piece of common ground—the "persona" or attributive convention—shows its firm strength by appearing in many forms, some of them glancing and implicit, like Lowell's lines:

> at the dedication
> William James could almost hear the bronze Negroes
>   breathe.

Others are outright, and explicitly dramatic, as the historical monologues and dialogues of Richard Howard. Or, there is Berryman's Henry, who is autobiographical enough to reminisce about Berryman's actual friends and locales, yet at the same time is "not the poet, not me"—as Berryman says in a prefatory snatch of his own voice.

The special and strange nature of this technique, from a point of view outside modernism, can be suggested by considering two such moments of a poet speaking—in preface—as personally and undramatically as Ben Jonson spoke in his own voice, in his verses. On the one hand, there is the "not me" statement by Berryman, prefatory to the intimate, sincere book *The Dream Songs*, with its many detailed references to actual people. On the other hand, there is Richard Howard's prefatory dedication to his *Untitled Subjects*, which invites us to read those Victorian monologues in the light of Browning's line "I'll tell my state as though 'twere none of mine."

These two disclaimers are explicit or implicit in much modern writing: that the statement by or about oneself is only seemingly a personal statement in words; and, conversely, that the seemingly objective "character" in fact presents a statement about oneself. The underlying ideas about ambivalence, indirection, and drama are so pervasive that we tend to receive them as immutable and immemorial. Such peculiar and familiar statements as those by Berryman and Howard suggest both the range and the unity of the ground in question. The convention or illusion that the poet can at once say, yet somehow not-say, is behind both statements. We accept that convention or illusion because we know it well and because—though rationally it may be nonsense—it speaks to deep needs shared by writer and reader.

II. Lowell

Robert Lowell's "For the Union Dead" is a meditative poem that for some readers may seem relevant to the idea of persona only on Procrustean terms. But the technique is used effectively and repeatedly, with a deft reliance on the reader's familiarity with its principles. The lines

> at the dedication
> William James could almost hear the bronze Negroes
> breathe

do not simply tell us something about William James, or the time and place embodied by him; they also permit Lowell to use or incorporate a figure of speech, and some diction, which he needs but would rather not use in his own voice: that the bronze Negroes seemed to breathe presents an ideal vital to the poem but hard for Lowell to talk about.

And in relation to William James himself, Lowell can suggest possible reservations about dedication to the idea that the violent death of the actual men behind the statue was redeemed or justified. Wistfully respecting that idea, the poet, beholding the statue propped up against the vibrations of construction for an underground car park, also feels bound to question it. In other words, a range of ambivalence is defined, to degrees that we understand rather precisely, and admire, because we know how to read such writing.

This is not the "influence" upon Lowell of Eliot's

(The lengthened shadow of a man
   Is history, said Emerson
Who had not seen the silhouette
   Of Sweeney straddled in the sun)

but rather an instance of writing that shares and inherits some of Eliot's concerns and ways of writing and, most of all, the ways of reading that result.

The process of attribution permeates "For the Union Dead," to the point of quotation marks included in an attribution more equivocal than the first:

Shaw's father wanted no monument
except the ditch,
where his son's body was thrown
and lost with his "niggers."

And another passage, in a play on words, supplies a phrase that identifies Lowell's complex relation to these Boston abolitionists, their language and their feelings:

He is out of bounds now. He rejoices in man's lovely,
peculiar power to choose life and die—
when he leads his black soldiers to death,
he cannot bend his back.

Unbound and freed by his confident death, Colonel Shaw also embodies a moral attitude that is not so much rejected as "out of bounds now," an optimism or heroism—and a racial attitude?—untenable for the poet-spectator who regards Shaw's statue, the fence, the steamshovels, his television set, the demanding cars that represent a "savage servility" difficult to abolish.

For tortuously complex reasons, the poet must evoke an ideal for contrast, and must admire it without professing it. He must imply, with utmost tact bordering on reticence, a comparison between the moral consequences of depending upon slavery and the moral consequences of depending upon gross machines. The point here is, first, that the poet's goals are, indeed, such tact and indirection; second, that he manages the task with brevity and grace by using a device his readers know so well that they hardly notice it. Attribution, quotation, borrowing of terms, allusion to what someone else hears, sees, said, or might have said—for Lowell these are ways to qualify or refine ironies and allegiances.

Without trying to treat even this one poem as a whole, one can observe that lines like those about the "bronze Negroes" suggest the general tone and subject of failed sympathy: spectatorhood. This modest, rather self-chastising subject also pervades the poems of *History,* sometimes under the guise of a seeming "topicality." Not denying the authentic topicality of those remarkable poems, or otherwise judging them, I would like to point out two aspects of the poems in *History:* the actual or implied quotation marks, sometimes surrounding whole poems, and the peculiar ambivalence of the volume, especially in its later poems.

A prominent instance is the poem that begins "It was at My Lai or Sonmy or something," and ends:

> "Lieutenant LaGuerre said, 'Shoot her.' I said,
> 'You shoot her, I don't want to shoot no lady.'
> She had one foot in the door. . . . When I turned her,
> There was this little one-month-year-old baby
> I thought was her gun. It kind of cracked me up."

("WOMEN, CHILDREN, BABIES, COWS, CATS")

The poem is entirely enclosed between quotation marks. It may seem strange to suggest that such material is subjected to a systematic and pervasive ambivalence; "ambivalence" may not be precisely right, but whatever we call the attitude, Lowell seems to have undertaken the problem of atrocity precisely as a challenge to that sadly reflective attitude. It is hard to find words for what I perceive to be the poem's attitude toward most of the serious emotions raised—*potentially*—by the poem, the horror, fear, and need to condemn: these feelings are not exactly dismissed, but they are left to go without saying. We are not allowed to elaborate them, or even to concentrate upon them.

What we are allowed to feel in fairly elaborate detail and fluctuation are, first, the speaker's confusion, and then his peculiar, distinct dignity. But beyond the limits and somewhat unexpected contours of the speaker's character is the subject of remembering: how the dead possess our remembering, the small good it does them, and how accidental and sadly bewildering the contact is between historical actions and individual character.

These remarks may seem to neglect the poem's other, historical material: the American war-making in Indochina, and what it did to Indochinese and to Americans; but a similarly unhistorical and reflective emphasis is suggested by the poems before and after this one in *History*. "Remembrance Day, London 1970's" finds the poet looking for notices of his new book in the Sunday papers, where he finds instead tokens of mortality and remembrance and remembrance's limits. And perhaps the most penetrating of these tokens of vanity appears not in the newspaper, but as a slip of paper in the poet's coat: announcing a memorial evening—vain? futile?— for a poet whose work will not be found reviewed or remembered in the newspaper.

The third poem, "Identification in Belfast," also has to do with the traditional theme of vanity or futility—with what may be Lowell's special twist of gloomy comedy, the possibility that our futilities may be our most memorable or essential parts. A person's frailties may be more enduring than the frail bits of paper meant to memorialize larger claims on memory. "Identification" is spoken (except for three lines, about rubber bullets and children, in Lowell's own voice) by a father who identifies the dead body of his son by means of the son's trick matches that, as the father strikes them one by one, will not light. This is no less a token of absurdity, and no less convincing, than the things one says:

> "When they first showed me the boy, I thought oh good,
> it's not him because he is a blonde—
> I imagine his hair was singed dark by the bomb."

Or even more arbitrary, foolish, true at the same time:

"The police were unhurried and wonderful,
    they let me go on trying to strike a match . . ."

"Wonderful" and "oh good" have the same unexpected appeal,
a sort of dignified humility or graceful silliness, as the word
"lady" for the murdered My Lai victim. The same quality, hu-
mane and unhistorical as the clowns in a Shakespeare history-
play, pervades the solemnly marching veterans in the first poem
of these three, "Remembrance Day, London 1970's":

The remembered live, bagpipers in tan kilts,
    their old officers in black suit, bowler and poppy,
    their daughters on the sidewalk keeping their step.

The phrase "the remembered live," which seems to introduce a
conventional profundity, turns into something funnier and
more complexly touching.

So by a variety of means—context within the volume for
example, and from that context reference to broad traditional
themes like "all is vanity"—Lowell manages to convey a many-
sided attitude, largely through quotation. The vanity of life and
life's remembrances—one's book, daughters and fathers, pow-
ers (the doomed runner Lillian Board, the poet) and idiosyn-
crasies—are as movingly ineffective as trick matches, rubber
bullets (which can be ineffectively "humane"), memorial pop-
pies and pamphlets, our inherited soft or genteel diction ("I
don't want to shoot no lady. . . . It kind of cracked me up").

This is not a poem that "contains history," then, in Pound's
definition of the epic; rather, it is historical elegy, like the Anglo-
Saxon poem "The Ruin": a meditation located in the places and
voices and characters of history as though they constituted a

landscape. We are familiar with this tradition. Unlike, say, Marvell's "Horatian Ode" or Gogol's *Dead Souls*, Lowell's work does not present particular rulers, states, or peoples as of the first urgency: instead, they are there because they are ruined or ruinous, and so conduct the meditation of death and remembrance to deeper levels. It is extraordinary that Lowell can write such a poem about such "topical" material. In part, the reason he can write it and we can read it lies in "The Waste Land" and Canto LXXXI, and beyond them perhaps earlier salvagings of wisdom or repose from historical ruin, like Lionel Johnson's "By the Statue of King Charles at Charing Cross" and Browning's invented Italy. The mode goes back at least to Samuel Johnson's version of Juvenal, but the method and the feeling belong to the modernist tradition.

To speak less sweepingly, Lowell uses the dramatic technique as a means of caution and melancholy remove. Whether extended or rapid and indirect, reliance on views and voices other than the poet's own indicates hesitance, an often gloomy preoccupation with failed sympathy. The ruin of history not only suggests mortality, it also forces the role of inert spectator upon one: spectator both of history itself and of its shady offspring News. At first, the following poem seems more straightforward, and perhaps even more straightforwardly topical:

Aswan Dam

Had Pharaoh's servants slaved like Nasser's labor,
Egyptian manhood under Russian foremen,
the pyramid. . . . I saw the Russians and imagined
they did more tangible work in a day than all Egypt. . . .

Dr. Mohammed Abdullah Fattah al Kassas
fears the Dam will slow the downstream current,
dunes and sandbars no longer build up buffers
along the Delta and repulse the sea—
the Mediterranean will drown a million farms,
wild water hyacinths evaporate Lake Nasser,
snails with wormlike bloodflukes slide incurably
to poison five hundred miles of new canals. . . .
Rake-sailed boats have fished the fertile Nile;
Pharaoh's death-ship come back against the shore.

But the eight-line attribution is essential, not incidental. For the man whose many, unmistakably traditional names Lowell relishes, the High Dam's ecological bad effects constitute, simply, a vivid disaster to come. The four lines preceding the attribution and the sonnet "couplet" following it suggest a much different attitude. The location-shifting modern technologists with their efficient empire appear to exceed the historical native empire in the area of "tangible work." The tone is too neutral and musing at this point to say that the phrase "tangible work" is ironic, but the fifth line, with its incantation of a name, suggests that possibility. And then the description of unforeseen derangement proceeds, increasingly less neutral and more charged in tone.

This incurable poisoning is reflected upon oddly by the final lines, the poet's response to the indirect quotation that has made up most of the poem. An historical observation linked by a semicolon to a peculiarly seer-like last line:

Rake-sailed boats have fished the fertile Nile;
Pharaoh's death-ship come back against the shore.

These lines present the predicted engineering and biological calamity—*if* it should come—as a reassertion or victory of the ancient past: a past not only feared for its persisting fatal power, but respected for its sinister dignity. But the disaster is only what Dr. Fattah al Kassas fears; could the lines be read in a second sense, dismissing those fears in the enormous context of time? Or as a kind of perverse, self-destructive wishful thinking on the part of an ancient culture divided and invaded by a new one?

In the first sense, antiquity is allied with the natural world in a kind of revenge delivered upon the clever innovators and their projects. The optimism of multiplied tangible works is frustrated by the working of dark laws whose calamity seems nearly to satisfy the poet. But even in the second sense—that the prediction is wrong, and perhaps rooted in national feelings—a figurative longing remains, for some alliance between the ancient past and the physical setting of the terrain.

The effect of the reference to antiquity is to evoke an attitude toward such natural laws that is conservative, cautious, pessimistic. The poet's brooding sympathy is with the builders and with the man who criticizes them, as it was with the American soldier and the victim. But again that sympathy is limited or cut short, by a sense less of history than of time and ruin. Lowell is sure only that history and the physical world are allied, contingent, and ominous. The Russian engineers and their critic both seek to "contain" history by understanding the past and planning the future; but Lowell, remote and given to second thoughts, returns to the attitude of elegy, and qualification.

That qualification arises from a remarkably intricate play between the six lines in the poet's own voice—for instance, what he "imagined"—and the image of disaster attributed to another voice. We participate in a highly sophisticated technique and, with an illusion of relatively little effort, feel the poet's tentative, oblique relation to history and historical judgments.

History—or perhaps I should say "the past"—has a long-standing association with the post-Romantic ways of using a dramatic speaker. The nineteenth-century origins often involve a fascinated borrowing from the past of its belief, its fanaticism or wholehearted passion, vicarious emotional riches. Beginning perhaps with Landor, this stream includes Browning's fancy-dress Italian Renaissance and the English obsession with southern Catholicism echoed by such poems as Ernest Dowson's "Carthusians" or Lionel Johnson's "Our Lady of the Snows."[2] The knights and troubadours of William Morris or of the early Ezra Pound seem to share in this reliance on the emotional life—more lucid or more approachable or of greater conviction?—of a largely invented past. The tradition is itself used as material in the rich folds of Richard Howard's *Untitled Subjects*. Different as Lowell's book is, he is linked to this line by the way he conducts the emotional battle between doubt and sympathy, with a rhetoric of attribution.

III. Berryman

To assign part of the poem to a voice or protagonist gives the attributed element a kind of autonomy, however illusory or conventional. Lowell has used that illusion of autonomy as a way to approach elusive or ambivalent judgments of outward matters, values of a cultural or social kind. In John Berryman's poems dramatic devices often seem to work similarly in relation to more wholly inward judgments; the quasi-autonomous element in the poem supplies a way to have one's self-dramatization and yet to judge it—or at least to stand a little apart from it. (Ted Hughes's *Crow* seems to carry this principle even further.)

Stylistically, persona or attribution works for Lowell largely as a way to balance meanings and allegiances in complex masses: in line, sentence, paragraph. As adapted to Berryman's meanings, the equally elaborate screens and attributions seem to free the poet mainly in the matter of diction—making legitimate particular words that in the single authorial voice might be too disparate or flat or maudlin.

So, though the syntactical eruptions of baby talk or minstrel-talk may seem to have some particular, special implication, Berryman's language seems to me to grow first of all from the poet's need for a vocabulary that does not restrict him or embarrass him. And weight and strength therefore depend not on the words, in a way, but on areas between the words, on the disparities and oddball vacuums:

> ... close by a smothering southern sea
> spreadeagled on an island by my knee.
> —You is from hunger, Mr. Bones,
>
> I offers you this handkerchief, now set
> your left foot by my right foot,
> shoulder to shoulder, all that jazz,
> arm in arm, by the beautiful sea,
> hum a little, Mr. Bones.
> —I saw nobody coming, so I went instead.

(THE DREAM SONGS, 76)

Perhaps the most important point to be made is that the colloquial words and the gag-words are not the words for which the extravagant style provides a kind of license or passport. Rather, the colloquial words help the syntax, the gags, and the personae in a general effort to admit another kind of phrase—like "a smothering southern sea"—just as in ordinary talk tough-slangy taglines such as "all that jazz" often excuse and qualify a phrase the speaker fears may seem too elevated or pretentious.

But "elevated or pretentious" does not exactly identify the kind of language that I mean, that I think Berryman originally felt driven to use by his material, and that in turn demanded his method. This kind of language has tended to be driven out of modern poetry by various pressures: the pressure toward evocative physical description as being the most essentially poetic use of language; the pressure toward idiomatic, spoken discourse. The result of these is to put extraordinary, cramping demands for freshness upon those words—mostly by necessity "abstract"—which in the ordinary way name the emotions themselves directly; so, in passages like the following one, the assumed voices and mannerisms provide a more or less ironic context for late-Romantic diction like "proud," "strike . . . from despair," "polished women," "dream awhile," "flashing and bursting":

> Something about this
> unshedding bulky bole-proud blue-green moist
>
> thing made by savage & thoughtful
> surviving Henry
> began to strike the passers from despair

so that sore on their shoulders old men hoisted
six-foot sons and polished women called
small girls to dream awhile toward the flashing &
    bursting tree!

(THE DREAM SONGS, 75)

But it is precisely only the context that is ironic, the weird man-ner. The irony is only that of a man in pain assuming dialects and self-effacing tones in torments of embarrassment and dif-fidence, as to distract himself. That is, the phrases of celebra-tion, and the poet's phallic pride in his book, are meant; the irony constitutes a sort of request for permission to use such phrases and to express such pride.

To put it another way, the "thing made" represents a return to the more or less late-Romantic idea of the poem as an irre-sistible outpouring, an emotional need and lifting-up for writer and reader; but while in some ways an idea like that one has come round again, largely replacing the mandarin, new-critical ideas about composition, it is also true that the standards of language that belong to the period of Eliot and Stevens retain their strength. For the subject of pain and survival Berryman, in *The Dream Songs,* wanted a fluent, ready language that could cover ground rapidly, establishing feelings without laborious "objective correlatives" and meticulously "sculpted" phrases. The Swinburnian "smothering southern sea" of 76 and the ad-jectival passage of the "six-foot sons" in 75 are the essential tongue of the poems, a sort of forbidden or ritual language ad-mitted by the surface lingo of the dream-song manner.

In fact, there is a temptation to see much of modern poetry's history as a series of strategies for retaining or recovering the elevation of Victorian diction. I am thinking less of the nineties-ish moments in Pound and Eliot than of such phrases of aroused and bardic diction as:

> An eagle rejoices in the oak trees of heaven

(JAMES WRIGHT, "TODAY I WAS SO
HAPPY I MADE THIS POEM")

> We shall see the grave of love as a lovely sight and
>   temporary
>   near the elm that spells the lovers' names in roots

(FRANK O'HARA, "ODE TO JOY")

> It is true
> That only flesh dies, and spirit flowers without stop.

(GALWAY KINNELL, "FREEDOM, NEW HAMPSHIRE")

The tones of the forbidden language of Arnold and Tennyson, against which modernism (according to one view) reacted, sometimes appear more or less explicitly, as in the last lines of the first Dream Song:

> Once in a sycamore I was glad
> all at the top, and I sang.
> Hard on the land wears the strong sea
> and empty grows every bed.

This same note, similarly associated with a bardic renewing of the past through poetry, appears in Pounds's early, pre-Raphaelite poems like "Ballateta" or even, briefly, in the rhymes and diction of "Ash Wednesday":

The new years walk, restoring
Through a bright cloud of tears, the years, restoring
With a new verse the ancient rhyme. Redeem
The time. Redeem
The unread vision in the higher dream
While jewelled unicorns draw by the gilded hearse.

But for Berryman the use (however ironic) of the old poetic
diction is not archaizing or momentary. He establishes the con-
text for it and then makes it into a readily available poetic lan-
guage whose aim is largeness of feeling: to make up in copious-
ness and range what it may lack in distinction of other kinds.
His subjects—disillusion, remorse, yearning, a despairing ir-
ritation with boundaries—demanded the somewhat sloppy
richness of the forbidden tongue.

The point may be more persuasive if I quote all of Dream
Song 29 (which seems to me to be one of the most successful)
and ask the reader to make a kind of imaginary revision, remov-
ing Henry and the eccentric syntax, but retaining the words and
images and their approximate order—conceiving also, if pos-
sible, a background murmur of Tennysonian figures of sound:

There sat down, once, a thing on Henry's heart
so heavy, if he had a hundred years
& more, & weeping, sleepless, in all them time
Henry could not make good.
Starts again always in Henry's ears
the little cough somewhere, an odour, a chime.

And there is another thing he has in mind
like a grave Sienese face a thousand years

would fail to blur the still profiled reproach of. Ghastly,
with open eyes, he attends, blind.
All the bells say: too late. This is not for tears;
thinking.

But never did Henry, as he thought he did,
end anyone and hacks her body up
and hide the pieces, where they may be found.
He knows: he went over everyone, & nobody's missing.
Often, he reckons, in the dawn, them up.
Nobody is ever missing.

It is true that the approach I suggest is not fair as a whole judgment of the poem; to call attention to the possibility

Often he reckons them up in the dawn

does not necessarily prove a great deal about the line as actually written. I suggest the exercise to make only a restricted, but important, point: namely, that a contemporary poet has adapted an elaborate mannerism in order to speak simply, that he uses one part of his tradition (the intricate use of a strange speaker) to make available another part of it. That other part, the late-Romantic feeling of the diction, is made clear by a process of mutilation for which I apologize. Anyway, here is a rough outline of the imaginary revision that I suggest as an experiment:

. . . so heavy that if I had a hundred years
And more of weeping, sleepless, in all that time
I could not make it good. Always in my ears
There starts again somewhere an odour, a chime. . . .

> . . . thing in my mind whose still profiled reproach,
> Like a grave Sienese face, a thousand years
> Would fail to blur. . . .

The quaint or grotesque nineteenth-century writer so suggested is not Berryman, of course. To isolate his diction in a context that may suggest its origins does, however, help to define the method of *The Dream Songs*.

The essence of the poem is the violently tormenting regret and guilt; no tears, no madness or violence or vision, will expiate that torment:

> All the bells say: too late.

In fact, it is not only too late, but too far or too deep, too undramatizable perhaps. Too far beyond action, anyway. In themselves, the Romantically broad emotional terms might imply some outcome of the feeling in the world of action. But Henry, the specialized ironic twitches of dream-song argot, the strange ways of the poem, all imply that this feeling is beyond or apart from action or even dramatic expression. The poet is permanently burdened with the pent-up nature of the feeling, and the style of the poem represents a kind of husk of being, surrounding the emotional essence. The dry, hard sense of circumstance and limit, which seems to rule out tears as well as atrocity, condemns the poet to insomniac meditation. The pressure against such limits creates the oddity of his voice.

The term for a cloak so involved, so egregious, and so arbitrary from some points of view is "mannerism." The vital, difficult question about *The Dream Songs* is whether the manner is finally arbitrary, or justified in some way oblique yet profound.[3]

IV. Hardy, Ransom, Berryman

Leaving aside any ultimate judgments about *The Dream Songs* as a whole, the time has come to show more specifically how actual language in contemporary poems can be related to the language of poems earlier in the modernist tradition. I want to use the poetic style of Thomas Hardy as a kind of pitch pipe, in order to bring together lines by Hardy, Berryman, and John Crowe Ransom. For me, the collocation helps define the tone and motive of particular strange moments, in all three writers, as self-deflation: an impatience with certain elegant and long-standing ways of writing that the poet has mastered but mistrusts. The test of this idea must be quotation, with comparison of how the apparently similar passages work in their context.

Readers more or less expect Hardy to take such headlong risks as the word "flock" applied to the people in the first stanza of "The Oxen" or the oddly downright location of the dead woman as "—elsewhere—" in "Beeny Cliff." These bold or violent thrusts of diction are similar in their effect to the even more strikingly odd grammatical inversions and prosodic enjambments, like the phrase "lippings mere" at the end of a line in the poem "Nature's Questionings." Above all, Hardy's poems convey, repeatedly, a sense of collision: colloquial language banging against formal or archaic language; innocence alternating suddenly with elegance; a ballad-like surface broken by totally different kinds of utterance. The purpose of such strategies is clearest in the irony—comedy, even—of a poem like "He Inadvertently Cures His Love Pains." The title alone suggests

Berryman—and the lightly sardonic wit of the poem itself (singing rhymes, macabre diction, self-mockery, dialogue) seems midway between Dream Song and Landor epigram.

As the purpose of Hardy's collisions and quirks becomes more complex, the feelings that arise from the poems are a sense of glibness and a conflicting sense of anguish—a pairing that collide forcefully in this poem:

A Drizzling Easter Morning

And is he risen? Well, be it so. . . .
And still the pensive lands complain,
And dead men wait as long ago,
As if, much doubting, they would know
What they are ransomed from, before
They pass again their sheltering door.

I stand amid them in the rain,
While blusters vex the yew and vane;
And on the road the weary wain
Plods forward, laden heavily;
And toilers with their aches are fain
For endless rest—though risen is he.

The contrasting spiritual glibness and spiritual anguish that are the poem's materials express themselves on the level of language in the glibness of such verses as

While blusters vex the yew and vane,

which is all but comically fluent—and, on the other hand, in the grammatical agony of the poem's last phrase. The strain of the grammatical inversion "risen is he," like the strain in the archaic run-over word "fain," is a strain that almost parodies the elegance and ease of rhymes and inverted periods. The plain and conversational element in the poem—"I stand amid them in the rain"—seems doubting and ironic about aspects of the verse line, of Victorian rhetoric, just as the speaker is doubting and ironic, reluctantly, about the Christian myth. In neither case is the object of doubt completely rejected.

A similar air of grotesquerie, or of talking through closed teeth, arises from the extraordinary figure of speech: the dead men wait in their graves as if wondering nervously whether to sacrifice the security of home for the social activity beyond the front door. The strange "ransomed" complicates this sense of the inappropriate. One word that comes to mind as descriptive of the whole is "sardonic." That word also describes a poem like 56 from *The Dream Songs*:

> Hell is empty. O that has come to pass
> which the cut Alexandrian foresaw,
> and Hell lies empty.
> Lightning fell silent where the Devil knelt
> and over the whole grave place hath settled awe
> in a full death of guilt.
>
> The tinchel closes. Tenor, & plunging, swipes.
> I lay my ears back. I am about to die.
> My cleft feet drum.
> Fierce, the two-footers club. My green world pipes
> a finish—for us all, my love, not some.
> Crumpling, I—why,—

So in his crystal ball them two he weighs,
solidly, dreaming of his sleepy son,
ah him, and his new wife.
What roar solved once the dilemma of the Ancient of
　　Days,
what sigh borrowed His mercy?—Who may, if
we are all the same, make one.

Berryman in *The Dream Songs* repeatedly constructs a gro-
tesque contrast between personal or social realities and loftier,
more traditional concerns. In this poem, the obverse of Hardy's,
the idea that Hell is empty and the old theologies outgrown is
presented with a sonorous, semi-parodied glibness, analogous
to the glibness of "blusters vex the yew and vane":

　　Lightning fell silent where the Devil knelt.

And then, in the second stanza, the tormented syntax and ar-
chaism modulate into a more deeply considered passage. The
relatively facile "full death of guilt" is succeeded by a first-
person passage, in which the Pan-like Devil-poet uses language
that is expressive in a clenched manner comparable to Hardy's
"risen is he" and "fain":

　　The tinchel* closes. Terror, & plunging, swipes.

To complete the parallel, the plain tones of specific, local reality
(like "I stand amid them in the rain") counterpoints the grander
diction with the quiet insistence of the ordinary:

---

* "tinchel" = "a closing circle of hunters" (O.E.D.).

solidly, dreaming of his sleepy son,
ah him, and his new wife.

The inaudible or jangling rhymes, like the "hath" and "ah," are part of an intricate, unsettled doubt. As Hardy's concluding lines complete a sardonic doubting of a theology that he would also like to entertain, Berryman's last lines doubt, with similarly grim, mixed feelings, the idea that a theology is obsolete:

What roar solved once the dilemma of the Ancient
    of Days,
what sigh borrowed His mercy?—Who may, if
we are all the same, make one.

This is "modern poetry" in one of its main aspects. Pushing ahead through the terms and sonorities, a negative, irritable quality develops the poem: tempering those terms with the particular realities of the rain, or the sleepy son; disclaiming the sonorities with a kind of tortured catch in the voice.

At times in Hardy the effect of such a style is to present the poet's need for toughness or moral detachment. He may in some poems seem equally impatient with the voices of elegance and innocence both, abrading them against one another. What critical description, for example, can we apply to the effect of the weird triple rhymes in "Ten Years Since"?

And the trees are ten feet taller,
And the sunny spaces smaller
Whose bloomage would enthrall her;
And the piano wires are rustier,
The smell of bindings mustier,

The lofts and lumber dustier
Than when, with casual look
And ear, light note I took
Of what shut like a book
    Those ten years since!

The superb execution of this perverse undertaking holds back
the reader's first judgment that the form is the result of bad
taste, a lapse or experiment. But if it is not bad taste, then it
must be a kind of grimace, a gesture of apology or expiation for
writing a poem at all, about such feelings. The verse questions
its own artifice by exaggerating it. The formality of rhyme and
refrain underscores the somewhat ludicrous difference between
the man who writes in the present and the man in the past who
suffered unaware the "casual" unformed progress of moral
events. The slightly flawed parallelism of "casual look and ear"
recall similar pairings by Berryman, who also wrote "My lass is
braking. My brass is aching" (Dream Song 13)—and though
that clowning is extreme, barroom-burlesque, both Henry and
Hardy's speaker are simultaneously literary, and anti-literary.

This disturbed, skeptical, thrashing manner in Hardy has
been called "the language of lost order" by Samuel Hynes.[4] It is
hard to say what the more extreme manner, the heavier freight
of ironic misgivings, should be called in Berryman, where not
only order but even single subjects seem lost in a swarm of leer-
ing or weeping distractions. When he would speak of death, for
example, various social or historical contexts seem to threaten
the very dignity of the subject.

There is another way to approach such moments. In both
poets, they suggest a desire to deal with the materials and

voices, all at once, of the novel, the meditation, the ballad, the lyric, the occasional verse, even the epic or verse romance. In other words, Hardy—no less than Berryman—often writes like a man looking for a way to deal with those compound states of feeling associated with the modernist rhetoric of Pound and Eliot. In brutal summary, we could characterize that modernist style as oblique, shifting, subtly dramatic, allusive, frequently "musical" or associational in structure, sometimes inscrutably imagistic. Hardy's style is not much like that. Treating similarly jarring contexts and conflicting feelings, perhaps with similar misgivings about traditional poetic languages, Hardy writes in a way that is direct, persistent, without subtle dramatic mask, not often allusive, essentially traditional in structure and prosody, more symbolic than inscrutable in image. So, we must see him as representing another, alternate version of anti-Tennysonian poetic language:[5] for poetic modernism, no less than Hardy's style, could be described from the Victorian point of view by Hynes's phrase, "the language of lost order."

To suggest two historical extremities of the process that finds language for lost order, and to show some of the continuities in that process, I want to compare another poem by Berryman with Matthew Arnold's poem "Self-Dependence." "Self-Dependence" exemplifies some forms of language and statement that *The Dream Songs* use, using them in order to reject them.

Arnold begins, "Weary of myself, and sick of asking/ What I am and what I ought to be." Standing at a ship's prow, he addresses the "starlit sea" and the stars, which have "calmed" him since childhood; he asks the stars and the sea to let him feel his soul "becoming vast like you." In response, an answer comes from "the intense, clear, star-sown vault of heaven,/ Over the lit sea's unquiet way," advising the poet "Wouldst thou *be* as they are? *Live* as they." The final four stanzas, in theme and language, may illuminate certain aspects of Berryman's manner and subject; the lofty speech and shadowy substance of Arnold's moralizing good cheer almost force the reader to wince ironically:

> "Unaffrighted by the silence round them,
> Undistracted by the sights they see,
> These demand not that the things without them
> Yield them love, amusement, sympathy.
>
> "And with joy the stars perform their shining,
> And the sea its long, moon-silvered roll;
> For self-poised they live, nor pine with noting
> All the fever of some differing soul.
>
> "Bounded by themselves, and unregardful
> In what state God's other works may be,
> In their own tasks all their powers pouring,
> These attain the mighty life you see."
>
> Oh air-born voice! Long since, severely clear,
> A cry like thine in mine own heart I hear:
> "Resolve to be thyself; and know that he,
> Who finds himself, loses his misery!"

Now here is Dream Song 14:

> Life, friends, is boring. We must not say so.
> After all, the sky flashes, the great sea yearns,

we ourselves flash and yearn,
and moreover my mother told me as a boy
(repeatingly) "Ever to confess you're bored
means you have no

Inner Resources." I conclude now I have no
inner resources, because I am heavy bored.
Peoples bore me,
literature bores me, especially great literature,
Henry bores me, with his plights & gripes
as bad as achilles,

who loves people and valiant art, which bores me.
And the tranquil hills, & gin, look like a drag
and somehow a dog
has taken itself & its tail considerably away
into mountains or sea or sky, leaving
behind: me, wag.

At first, the conjunction may seem pointlessly cruel to the poem by Arnold. However, Berryman's poem is more than parody; any cruelty in it is directed, in the end, at the poet's own impulses toward an easy "affirmation": the arbitrary optimism that may underlie a grandiloquent view of nature or the easily rolling rhythms of a certain style. (In some ways, the Arnold stanza beginning "And with joy" violates plain English syntax as much as any Dream Song.) To exaggerate that style, with its dignified verbs, broad abstract nouns, and Latinate grammar, and to deflate it with a colloquial counterpoint, is to beseech toughness or endurance of one's style. At the same time, the poet can use the style that annoys or embarrasses him, but that for some tasks he needs—needs more or less for its original, affirmative, purposes:

> will come in silence this distinguished one
> essaying once again the lower slopes
> in triumph, keeping up our hopes,
> and heading not for the highest we have done
> but enigmatic faces, unsurveyed,
> calm as a forest glade

(THE DREAM SONGS, 87)

In a way, this reclaiming of hoary verbal formula for sincere use is the converse of parody. In *The Dream Songs*, it relies upon a context that is like parody.

More characteristic is the sadly or savagely ironic mismating of traditional rhetoric with the language of grim local realities—in its simplest form, Berryman's mannerism of ending a line with "O" as in the lines "It's time to settle down-O" or "was Henry's gloomy Monday morning oh" (Dream Songs 332 and 134). (This habit of ironic anachronism recalls lines by Ransom ending in "alack" or his line about the dead girl's geese, "Who cried in Goose, Alas"; though the resemblance among the three poets rests upon more than such tricks, one can also mention Hardy's many uses of such ballad-derived gestures, as in the refrain to "During Wind And Rain.") But going beyond the mere use of archaic exclamations, nearly every Dream Song offers less trivial, more sustained examples of ironically "mismated" archaisms:

> Let's wander on the sands, with knitting bones,
> while the small waves please the poor seaweed
> so little.—The grand plough

distorts the Western Sky. Back to lurk!
We cannot rave ourselves. Let's hide. It's well
or ill,—there's a bell—so far,
the history of the Species: work, work, work.
All right, I'll stay. The hell with the true knell,
we'll meander as far as the bar.

(179)

My memory of his kindness comes like a flood
for which I flush with gratitude; yet away
he shouldna have put down Miss Trueblood.

(113)

For example, the two, rather opposed senses of "bar" in the last
line of 179 would be one—only "saloon," and not "impedi-
ment"—if the second, loftier sense were not reinforced by
phrases like "well or ill," "the true knell," and "the history of the
Species." In success or failure, this is the voice that finds elo-
quence of a certain kind necessary, yet intolerable: the bloated,
requisite backdrop of the Western Sky. The knots and disjunc-
tions are the voice's agony.

I hope that the comparison with Arnold will in itself suggest
some of the ways in which Berryman's collisions and mismar-
riages of language can work. Sometimes they serve as earnests
of the poet's discomfort with elegance, particularly the glib el-
egance of elegy and regret. Elegy and regret can become com-
fortable, just as the consolation of the natural world can—
through trumped-up spiritualization of a landscape—become
facile: "Oh air-born voice!" Verse itself, or natural description
itself, threatens to embody a false affirmation or grace, betray-

ing the absolute loss that is the poet's subject. In Hardy, and even more in Berryman, the sting of regret is shown as driving the poet forcibly through the various corridors of eloquence with a clumsily thrashing irritability.

How far the reader goes in accepting such a style and its demands—demands that at times are wholesale in *The Dream Songs*—is another, and difficult, question. My point here is the nature of those demands, the need to recognize them. Hynes quotes a monstrous line from Hardy's "At a Bridal," the eighth line below:

> When you paced forth, to await maternity,
> A dream of other offspring held my mind,
> Compounded of us twain as Love designed;
> Rare forms, that corporate now will never be!
>
> Should I, too, wed as slave to Mode's decree,
> And each thus found apart, of false desire,
> A stolid line, whom no high aims will fire
> As had fired ours could ever have mingled we;
>
> And, grieved that lives so matched should miscompose,
> Each mourn the double waste. . . .

The line is, in a sense, awful; in a sense it is merely the grotesque product of Hardy's search for a rhyme. But the poem is subtitled "Nature's Indifference." The speaker sees a woman, who seemed his destined mate according to nature, marry another man, an event that is hard for him to take; but those bitter reflections are nothing compared to the perception that follows. In the conclusion of the poem, he questions nature: why was this apparently "natural" match frustrated? The answer he imagines is, "That she [nature] does not care/ If the race all such sovereign types unknows." From the large, final perspective of "nature," the feelings and values that initiate the poem are meaningless.

In other words, the situation—ordinary enough in itself—is presented in such a way as to seem intolerable, as intolerable as the career of Hardy's Jude, or of Henry. And the language of "unknows" and "As had fired ours could ever have mingled we," of the scholastic "forms" and "corporate" jarring with the journalistic "Mode's decree," recalls the language of *The Dream Songs*—

The lust-quest seems in this case to be over

(163)

Most seem to feel
nothing is secret more
to my disdain I find, when we who fled
cherish the knowings of both worlds, conceal
more, beat on the floor. . . .

(88)

and, like that language, "Nature's Indifference" embodies the speech of a man who wants to convey that the elegance of rhyme and prolonged grammar contrasts with his experience—which is intolerable. This is the ironically ordered utterance of one who finds things "miscomposed." Instead of writing about chaos or disjuncture in a way that is chaotic or disjointed, the poet does the opposite: he writes in a way that is ironically learned or elegant or traditional, poking rhymes, verbs, and neologisms into strange places.

If the intolerable, in the form of guilt or frustration, is what we dream, because waking life cannot tolerate it, then the systematically discordant manner of using words is suitable to dreams—speech as bizarrely organized and as oddly appropriate as the dislocations and impossibilities of dreams. The two contrasted lines of descendants in "Nature's Indifference" are part of a waking dream of sorts.

The coinages and abrupt rhymes and odd-cobbled sentences of John Crowe Ransom may seem less dreamlike, less related to "intolerable" feelings or experiences, compared to the work of Hardy or to *The Dream Songs*. The pre-modernist poet and the poet devising a post-modernist style both seem more painfully gripped by experience, more sincerely disaffected with the (so to speak) Arnoldian elements in their own voice and spirit.

Yet the urbane, sardonic poems of Ransom share certain thematic concerns: the ubiquitousness and finality of death; the emptiness of regret; the eventual uselessness of natural beauty and of art. Ransom may be accused of seeking these grim materials to accommodate the sardonic style. But at its best, the style implies a justifying reservation, a confession that even verse becomes a sort of solemn clowning before the direness of life. The facts, presented in those curt final lines that often close a sentence with a lock-like rhyme, are such terribly simple facts that the art seems to blush for itself:

> It was a transmogrifying bee
> Came droning down on Chucky's old bald head
> And sat and put the poison. It scarcely bled,
> But how exceedingly

And purply did the knot
Swell with the venom and communicate
Its rigour! Now the poor comb stood up straight
But Chucky did not.

("JANET WAKING")

If the cruel archness of these lines—the polysyllabic words, the overblown grammar, the counterpoint of plain talk—is not directed against the little girl and her pet, they must be directed backward, at the grave poet who expects more from life than these simple facts, and who feels bound to speech. If the dry, droll elegance of "communicate," for example, parodies anything, it is poetry itself. As with Hardy and Berryman, these lines assert a quality of toughness (in contrast with a poem like "Self-Dependence") as well as a sense of the intolerable. This tone of toughness, rather than any matter of doctrine, may have motivated the early, old-fashioned objections to Hardy's "pessimism." Certainly it is important as a counterweight to the potentially maudlin materials and attitudes of Berryman—and in relation to the dead pets, children, gallants, and ladies of Ransom's poems.

It is worthwhile to compare the clinching last line above ("But Chucky did not") with the following from *The Dream Songs*:

So musing, they blew the whistle on the Cat,
Which was that.

(250)

They say the coffin closes without a sound
& is lowered underground!

(373)

The need not to flinch communicates its rigor. It is contrasted
with an urge toward the maudlin, and the contrast subsists in a
special region of the language, where extremes of urbanity and
awkwardness meet. The way that happens in Ransom's stanzas
on Chucky—wickedly flat rhymes, parodically formal syn-
tax—resembles the following stanza from Berryman's Dream
Song 106:

> Dogs fill daylight, doing each other ill:
> my own in love was lugged so many blocks
> we had to have a vet.
> Comes unrepentant round the lustful mongrel
> again today, glaring at her bandages & locks:
> his bark has grit.

"Transmogrifying" and "exceedingly" in Ransom's stanza play
against the flat click of the rhyme-words "head" and "bled"
somewhat as "unrepentant" and "lustful" above play against
"vet" and "grit."

Before quoting some similar passages from Hardy, here is an
incidental example (more gentle and inward) from the poet
who might serve as the earliest exemplar of the mode:

> The leaves are falling; so am I;
> The few late flowers have moisture in the eye;
> So have I too.

Scarcely on any bough is heard
Joyous, or even unjoyous, bird
  The whole wood through.

(WALTER SAVAGE LANDOR)

This laconic flirting with bathos becomes more or less grotesque in Hardy's hard-to-believe poem "Why She Moved House," which is subtitled "(The Dog Muses)":

And where she is she gets no sun,
  No flowers, no book, no glass;
Of callers I am the only one,
  And I but pause and pass.

The grotesque, ironic, horrible glibness of rhyme, image and sentence is even plainer, and more reminiscent of Ransom, in "Two Lips":

I kissed them in love, in troth, in laughter
  When she knew all; long so!
That I should kiss them in a shroud hereafter
  She did not know.

Something of the same tone—at times it seems to be a kind of preposterous *absence* of tone—becomes something extraordinary, if more muted, in the last stanza of Hardy's superb poem "My Spirit Will Not Haunt the Mound." The prominent rhymes, the casual word "jot" embedded in its Latinate grammatical inversion, the clipped, halting final two lines all grow from the eccentric coinage of the preceding stanza, the "ways" that were known "In backward days":

And there you'll find me, if a jot
        You still should care
For me, and for my curious air;
If otherwise, then I shall not,
        For you, be there.

This is perhaps a greater poem than anything in Ransom or Ber-
ryman, as Hardy is the greater poet. But a similarly muted ver-
sion of the style I have been discussing—a quieter or more con-
trolled sense of collision—appears in one of the most moving
of *The Dream Songs*, 145. The intricate rhymes become emphatic
in the last stanza; casual phrases like "—forgiveness time—" and
"an instant longer" and "what was needed" alternate with inver-
sions like "defeat sublime" or appear in complex sentences like
the final one. The run-over on "I'm" is not unlike the one on "jot"
in Hardy's poem; and as in Hardy's poem the movement of the
two closing lines is clipped, halting, qualified:

Also I love him: me he's done no wrong
for going on forty years—forgiveness time—
I touch now his despair,
he felt as bad as Whitman on his tower
but he did not swim out with me or my brother
as he threatened—

a powerful swimmer, to take one of us along
as company in the defeat sublime,
freezing my helpless mother:
he only, very early in the morning,
rose with his gun and went outdoors by my window
and did what was needed.

I cannot read that wretched mind, so strong
& so undone. I've always tried. I—I'm
trying to forgive
whose frantic passage, when he could not live
an instant longer in the summer dawn
left Henry to live on.

It seems to me to be more than coincidence that the similar styles—bringing elegance and formality into an ironic, hesitant relation with bluntness and strain—treat similar subjects, too: the complex thread of regret, guilt, longing, and illusion that connects the living with the dead. It is a subject both writers felt compelled to deal with in a way not too grandiloquent: personal, matter-of-fact at moments, yet protesting and pained; and they found similar solutions.

The element of parody, an emphasis upon the awkwardness of words, suggests a shared desire to preclude sentimentality. Ransom's "Lost Lady" also staves off that charge; the opening lines seem to have a Dream-Song inversion of grammar, and the second stanza, with its "clapping thunder," seems to have a Dream-Song mock-bombast:

This morning, flew up our lane
A timid lady bird to our birdbath
And eyed her image dolefully as death;
This afternoon, knocked on our windowpane
To be let in from the rain.

And when I caught her eye
She looked aside, but at the clapping thunder
And sight of the whole world blazing up like tinder

Looked in on us again most miserably,
Indeed as if she would cry.

The slyly comic self-dramatization is used by Ransom in the
first person:

Grim in my little black coat as the sleazy beetle,
And gone of hue,
Lonely, a man reputed for softening little,
Loving few—

("TOM, TOM, THE PIPER'S SON")

or, even more like Henry or like Hardy's "He Inadvertently
Cures His Love-Pains," in the third person:

Tell this to ladies: how a hero man
Assail a thick and scandalous giant
Who casts true shadow in the sun,
And, die, but play no truant.

The ironic grace and tortured syntax are surprisingly like the
idiom that Berryman reaches through the means, or occasion,
of his minstrel-dialect.

In other words, that dialect is more a means toward a style
than an end in itself (evoking the American South, or the stage,
or Blacks). If I am right about the style's uses, then it is signifi-
cant to find that similar emotional needs, in different writers,
have demanded similar poetic practices. It is also suggestive
that the particular ways of writing in question are discursive
rather than associational in structure; often grandly abstract in
diction; rather conservative in prosody; and often more explicit
than mysterious in figurative language.

That one must speak of affinity rather than "influence" seems to me to strengthen the point.[6] The archaisms and coinages and sentences twisted around demanding prosodic shapes all manifest the same distances and intimacies. The bizarre clots of words in Hardy, his inventions like "disesteeming" ("To Sincerity") spring from restraints and liberties similar to those of Ransom's line "And best bodiness to colorify" ("Painted Head"), just as the sardonic gentleness that is accorded to the dead or faded ladies of Hardy's "An Ancient to Ancients" resembles the feeling of Ransom's "Here Lies a Lady." And there are passages where the catchy, somewhat awkward movement, the alternately blunt and show-off diction, the laconic emotionalism, could nearly be from any of the three:

> Ah, the strict lovers, they are ruined now!
> I cried in anger. But with puddled brow
> Devising for those gibbeted and brave
> Came I descanting: Man, what would you have?

("THE EQUILIBRISTS")

What these voices share encompasses their difficulties of feeling and speech, as well as the general realm of their solving.

III. The Romantic Persistence

I. "Romantic": "Ode to a Nightingale"

Having looked at some specific texts by particular poets, I would like to approach the subject again in another, perhaps more theoretical, way.[1] Certain ideas and emotional conflicts suggest a continuity between contemporary and modernist poetry—and, beyond that, a continuity with the Romantic poetry of the nineteenth century. Monumental and familiar, the conflicts are between conscious and unconscious forces within the mind: between the idea of experience as unreflective, a flow of absolutely particular moments, and the reality of language as reflective, an arrangement of perfectly abstract categories.

It seems that every poet writing in English inherits these broad conflicts along with the language and other cultural goods. The poet also inherits responses to and assumptions about those conflicts, and I suspect that when a contemporary poem is a good one, then one can describe the poem's success by showing how the poet either understood those received ideas, recovering them from the area of mere mannerism, or else worked away from them altogether.

The way the essential Romantic conflicts persist and change can be shown by applying the terms of a great defining example—John Keats's "Ode to a Nightingale"—to modern and contemporary work. That poem, and especially its first, sixth, and seventh stanzas, can supply an especially clear and suggestive touchstone for the term "Romantic."

The first stanza is organized by the tightly logical transitions of lines five through seven. Though somewhat submerged in the luxurious figures of sound, and in the richly elaborated paradox (that "numbness pains"), this logical structure is explicit, nearly syllogistic:

> 'Tis not through envy of thy happy lot,
>> But being too happy in thy happiness,—
>>> That thou, light-winged Dryad of the trees, . . .

The pronoun part of the contraction " 'Tis" refers to the feeling that has gone before, and that these three lines define. The comma and dash, followed by the word "That," act as a colon introducing the explanation that follows.

So: the poet feels a peculiar emotion, unsettling but seductive, which consists of a loss of consciousness that is also an oversensitivity, an opiate that pains, a Lethean poison. This apparently irrational state becomes the object of the careful, even obsessively rationalistic distinction:

> 'Tis not through envy of thy happy lot.

Many of the misunderstandings and vulgarizations of the Romantic dilemma can be represented by the misreading of this line as though it said:

> 'Tis through envy of thy happy lot.

In fact, "it"—the feeling of the first four lines—has come about "through" too much of one kind of happiness, the poet's, which is caused by another, contrasting kind of happiness, the bird's.

That happiness—which the poet perceives with pleasure as well as pain, and that the poet feels moved to say he does not envy—is defined by the elegant long sentence that closes the stanza, the final chord of emphasis on the last word of all:

> thy happiness,—
> That thou, light-winged Dryad of the trees,
> In some melodious plot
> Of beechen green and shadows numberless,
> Singest of summer in full-throated ease.

That is, the poet's happiness is to be conscious of the bird's song, a song whose "happiness" is its ease—to be unconscious. The invisible bird merges with the "melodious" landscape, the two blending not only because the observer cannot distinguish them, but also because the bird in its ease does not distinguish itself and its song from the surrounding summer woods, as the poet must.

The poet must distinguish himself from the landscape because of his defining attributes: he is aware, he notices, he makes distinctions, he organizes his song into the rhymes, rhythms, and sentences that are a painstaking simulation of ease. The contrast between those abstract schemes that constitute his art and the blending continuum of tiny particulars that make up the natural world is a contrast named by Keats in a brilliantly suggestive phrase: "shadows numberless."

The shadows, dappled and overlapping, could not possibly be counted. As many as the leaves and even more dim, they are too many, too small, too indistinguishable. It is the poet, with his abstract, formulating intelligence, who even raises the question, as it is the poet who even raises the question of the pure birdsong "expressing" summer, or ease, or some humanly apprehensible "happiness." Like the shadows, the song is pure of that kind of meaning; it cannot be counted as expressing anything, unlike the elaborate "numbers" of Keats—the intricate patterns of his stanza.

These, then, are the terms of one principal strain of Romanticism, seen not as a doctrine but as a dilemma; in light of these terms, the conflicts of Keats's first four lines—the paining numbness, the sensuous poison—become less a paradox, and more the elements of a quandary. The Romantic poet is attracted, through intense perception, to dimness. The more actively the poet perceives the beloved natural world, the more alienated from it, for its quality is to perceive nothing. The more closely and lovingly the attentive poet enumerates separate natural details, the more distant the poet is from nature, for nature does not enumerate. Above all, the more we know about the "shadows numberless" or the "light-winged" bird, or the more we try to perfect that kind of knowledge in writing, the wider the gap between ourselves and the shadows and the bird, because their attractive essence is not to be conscious at all. In effect, it is this unconsciousness or "pure" being that Keats loves, and the more he knows and articulates the object of his love, the less like it he is.

These essential difficulties of the Romantic situation are multiplied if one is not simply a Romantic, but a Romantic poet. If what one loves and wishes to approach is embodied by unconscious being, by single phenomena as purely self-contained as the dappled shade or as the single, unreflecting moments of a birdsong, then the very calling of poetry is a problem. Every word is an abstraction, the opposite of a sensory particular; sentences are abstract arrangements, and the rhythms of verse like all rhythms are based upon the principle of recurrence, or form.

For these reasons, Keats can move from the double state with which he begins only *toward* the Lethe of the bird or the landscape. Though he seems later in the poem to arrive there, what I see as the firm moral base of the poem rejects that idea. Before returning to the text of the poem, it is necessary to say that the bird's song ("thy soul") is that part of nature's unreflecting continuum that seems most like human thought, though this is an illusion; and the act of the human mind that seems most like the self-contained, utterly particular being of the natural world is poetry. This seems true because the sentences and rhythms of poetry seem to embody that being as the mind ordinarily cannot. But this capacity of poetry is also an illusion; it is an illusion to the extent that abstract intelligence is in the nature of poetry, and in the nature of the mind itself.

The fading or dimness to which the poem repeatedly appeals is the haze of tiny discrete particulars, each clear and lucid in itself, just as each tiny, unreflecting fragment of time, if we could be conscious of it only, would become an eternity in itself. If consciousness, the faculty that places us in time by reflecting and generalizing, could be dissolved into its single elements, then we would command the ease of the nightingale and the summer.

The fourth stanza asserts that this dissolving of conscious intelligence can take place—indeed has taken place—through the power of poetry to concentrate on the details of sensory experience, leaving the quibbling and riddling brain behind. The dissolution is presented first as a kind of fairy tale:

> Already with thee! tender is the night,
>   And haply the Queen-Moon is on her throne,
>   Cluster'd around by all her starry Fays;
>   But here there is no light,
>   Save what from heaven is with the breezes blown
>   Through verdurous glooms and winding mossy ways.

The slightly negative air of these lines—a sense of vagueness or drunkenness or delusion—is deliberate, for the idea of dissolution, of becoming "like" the inanimate landscape, is rejected, attractive though it is.

It is rejected, first, implicitly, by the lovely fifth stanza, whose attractive appeal to the senses depends more and more upon names, and knowledge, and not simply upon the sense of smell, but upon the darkling poet's wit, and a nearly botanical precision:

> I cannot see what flowers are at my feet,
>   Nor what soft incense hangs upon the boughs,
> But, in embalmed darkness, guess each sweet
>   Wherewith the seasonable month endows
> The grass, the thicket, and the fruit-tree wild;
>   White hawthorn, and the pastoral eglantine;
>   Fast-fading violets cover'd up in leaves;
>   And mid-May's eldest child,
>   The coming musk-rose, full of dewy wine,
>   The murmurous haunt of flies on summer eves.

These splendid and scientific distinctions present the truth of the imagination—that it depends upon and works by the knowledge of time, of the times of things and the names of things, characteristic seasons, and haunts: generalities. The landscape thus known does not, itself, "guess" or generalize.

That implicit drawing-back from the mind's dissolution is made explicit in the next stanza, the sixth, which declares a grudging allegiance to consciousness using the logical method, and some of the diction, of the first stanza:

> Darkling I listen; and for many a time
>   I have been half in love with easeful Death,

—even in the dark, he is conscious, and the ease of being like the bird would be, for him as a human being, literal or figurative death. These blunt, harsh terms include one line that describes the fairy tale of the fourth stanza with its "Already with thee!":

>   Call'd him soft names in many a mused rhyme,

and the stanza closes with a final word as important as was "ease"—a kind of monosyllabic shock that completes the moral withdrawal from the delusions of the fourth stanza:

>   To take into the air my quiet breath;
>   Now more than ever seems it rich to die,
>   To cease upon the midnight with no pain,
>   While thou art pouring forth thy soul abroad
>   In such an ecstasy!
>   Still wouldst thou sing, and I have ears in vain—
>   To thy high requiem become a sod.

A sod. For consciousness to escape its loneliness and become like the unreflecting particulars of nature, which attract it, consciousness would have to die and become like a lump of earth. This death I take to be either literal or a state of mind.

In either case, Keats tells us, firmly, what is at stake in those desires that we sometimes express with such glib phrases as "merging with nature." To escape the loneliness of being the only creature who uses terms, who reflects, who speaks, who is conscious of time—the only creature who is *in* time as other than a succession of discrete instants—we would have to die. That forced loneliness, and the attraction of its opposite, the unconscious ease of the physical world, make up the motive force of the "Ode to a Nightingale."

To digress for a moment, some brief contemporary examples may help bring to mind the nature of that loneliness or separation. The lonely burden of consciousness—and not shame or violence—seems to me to be the true subject of W. S. Merwin, when, seemingly writing of shame and violence, he closes his poem "Avoiding News by the River" with a last line whose baldness is a sophisticated tactic:

> I am not ashamed of the wren's murders
> Nor the badger's dinners
> On which all worldly good depends
> If I were not human I would not be ashamed of
>   anything.

The need or problem here is to treat Keats's theme with no less sense of cost than Keats achieved. The solution is based on an elegantly shrugging simplification, an attempt to get back to the plainest roots of the situation.

The contemporary poet who carries this resource furthest may be Theodore Roethke. The rapt escapism of his late work is like the flight out of time by some impossibly naive contemporary of Keats:

> My breath grew less. I listened like a beast.

> ("HER BECOMING")

> The spirit says, you are nothing.

> ("WHAT CAN I TELL MY BONES")

The death or dissolving to nothing also means to become many, like the particles of breath dispersing on forest air, joining the undifferentiated details of landscape:

> A prisoner of smells, I would rather eat than pray.
> I'm released from the dreary dance of opposites.
> The wind rocks with my wish; the rain shields me;
> I live in light's extreme; I stretch in all directions;
> Sometimes I think I'm several.

> ("WHAT CAN I TELL MY BONES")

In judging such writing, it does not seem unfair to use the seriousness of Keats as a standard. My point for now is not how good or bad Roethke's poems or Merwin's are, but that the comparison is appropriate. When Suckling or Prior takes up the materials used by Donne and Greville, we make a comparison not simply of talent, but also of intellectual and moral grasp.

Returning to the "Ode," it is important to say that the theme of time, which I have been stressing, emerges most explicitly in the seventh stanza. The numberless particular fragments of nature, each different, are also numberless instants in time, each unique and without reference to what comes before or after. It is the poet's nature to organize these separate paradises, in effect contaminating them with his awareness of sequence, season, sentence, rhyme, connections of all kinds. Though the bird's song seems to express something like such a connecting and organizing soul, the bird's consciousness in fact simply *is* each moment of its song. That song does not vary from generation to generation, so there is nothing in the way of a soul there to die:

No hungry generations tread thee down.

If we ask, of the contrasting human generations, hungry for what? the answer must be as grand, and as embarrassing to say in a word, as "consciousness" or even "life." In terms of aware-ness, one nightingale is another, beings as identical as their songs, though they may be a hundred years apart. But even if I could understand perfectly every last nuance of John Keats's poem, even if it were a perfect poem, and even if all my life I did nothing but read it—even then only the tiniest glint of the ac-tual mind called John Keats would survive, a mere sliver of his consciousness. Indeed mind, which is a project in time, treads *itself* down as it roams from one state of mind in time to another.

That roaming or moving in time, attracted by the birdsong that seems to reconcile body and mind, *res* and *verba,* may em-bark on ventures as perilous and forlorn as the faery-vision of the fourth stanza. Those ventures are perilous because they embody a nostalgia for inert being, which for the mind is death; they are forlorn because they enforce the knowledge that consciousness is alone. It is alone in part because only consciousness can experience death, and the smaller death of each moment in time.

At no point, however, does the poet retract his declaration that he does not envy the bird; the nostalgia for unconsciousness, the nostalgic wish to live only in each unreflecting moment, is strong, but nevertheless it is firmly identified as a nostalgia for death. Anything else is a sorry delusion:

> . . . the fancy cannot cheat so well
> As she is famed to do, deceiving elf.

The complexity of conflicting truth and desire here is a caution against facile reference to "imaginative one-ness with nature" and similar phrases of "Romanticism" that sometimes appear in writing about poetry. For Keats, the situation is inherently, and not temporarily, a quandary: to be a "sod" or to be "forlorn."

One more digression into contemporary poetry may help clarify the rather large remarks about time and death in the last few paragraphs. Some of what I have written may seem to be mere fancy ideas or, worse, fancy talk: the kind of bland philosophizing about death and so forth that blights the practice of literary criticism. But the idea of nostalgia for unconsciousness has some intricate corollaries. Among these is the idea that death is an idea, an idea in time; in the natural realm that is unconscious of time (as we imagine it, anyway) there are a series of phenomena: a living body, a dead one. Note too, in this poem by Alan Stephens, how the relation of a single animal to the rest of his species echoes rather precisely the case of Keats's nightingale:

The Death of a Buffalo

Heavily from the shadeless plain to the river
The bull slants down and bends his head to draw
Bright water in, that goes unbroken ever.
He pauses, water threading from his jaw,
Impenetrably as he is, and old.
And, while the harsh beard drips and shines, the shore,
Beyond, grows flashing grasses. Through the cold
Water he lifts a foreleg, as before,
Showing the naked spot the ball drives through.
A shiver. The coming hour, the windy grass
Under the suns beyond him, these he knew,
Knows and shall know. They make no shift to pass
        Through death. Death is the elsewhere, an unwit
        Of the great body down, this side of it.

That which the animal's mind amounted to does not experience death; what he "knows" is the landscape as a succession of moments. Death is an idea in the poet's mind and the reader's, and not a demonstrable presence anywhere in the physical world of sun, wind, and body. The poem recalls Yeats's line: "Man has created death"; and that idea, or at least the idea that man has irrevocably discovered death, is implied by Stephens's poem. Behind that poem and behind the line I have quoted from Yeats lies the more general declaration of Keats: that man has created or discovered time itself, and so is doomed to live in it, forlorn.

Alone, exiled from the rest of the physical world by his consciousness that organizes, reflects, and articulates sensory particulars, the Romantic poet regards the natural world nostalgically, across a gulf that apparently can be crossed only by dying, either actually or through some induced oblivion. That gulf is closely related to the gulf between words and things. Various philosophical descriptions might apply to the situation. The broadest of these (if any such description is necessary) stems from the terms "nominalism" and "realism." Nominalism can be defined loosely as the doctrine that words and concepts are mere names, convenient counters of no inherent reality, though they may be useful means for dealing with the atomistic flux of reality. I understand philosophical realism as the opposite doctrine that universals—and, therefore, concepts and words—embody reality. The Romantic poet tends to look for values to emerge from particular experiences—associated sense perceptions and states of mind at particular moments—and insofar as that is true, he is a nominalist. But insofar as he is a poet he must to some extent be a realist, for those reasons that may bear repeating: words are abstractions, sentences are forms disposing their parts in time, and rhythm is based upon the concept of recurrence or pattern.

In Keats's terms, his fancy cannot quite delude him that it is possible to cross over, making his poetry into something as purely phenomenal and undeliberate as the nightingale's song. His painstakingly artful stanzas, his inventive diction, his unsettling awareness of time, prevent him from joining that unutterable realm. The very words he uses, because they are the most conscious part of him, recall his isolation from the landscape into which the bird so easily fades. Having defined the cost and the difficulty of reconciling his own nature with his nostalgia for unconscious nature, Keats suggests a hope or yearning in his final lines. Enormously qualified as it is, the idea of the fourth stanza is entertained again, if only as a question:

Was it a vision, or a waking dream?

By an illusion so controlled and exploited that it becomes a means of truth, the art of writing in verse can convey a sense of the contingent, beautifully unconscious sensory world. Can the conscious art of words moving in lines, the most physical aspect of language, somehow bridge the gulf with its rhythms, or is any such drawing closer merely an illusion? Can the poet's words about the world so unlike himself approach the objectivity of vision, or do they present only a waking dream?

These matters are hard to define, and as problems they are far from new. I raise them here to emphasize the double nature of the feeling that has one of its great embodiments in Keats's poem. First, the feeling is anti-intellectual, even anti-verbal. Second, that feeling is resisted, qualified, and to some extent rejected by Keats. Without denying what is beautiful and precious to him in the emotion, he suggests that it can be inimical to life. The complexity of his definition can be used to provide bounds and standards that apply to much or most of the poetry written in English since the time of Keats.

In part, the tradition involves a pressure to avoid or camouflage statement and abstraction. To invoke some terms, the act of predicating or generalizing violates the poet's nominalist sense of his experience as a stream of unique, particular perceptions. But insofar as he uses language with conviction, the poet must be a philosophical realist.

This uneasy relation with one's own medium has led Romantic and post-Romantic poets to devise remarkable ways of writing, which might make language seem less abstract and less discursive. The poem has pursued the condition of a thing.

This pursuit, for example, has played a motivating role in the development of the dramatic poem. In Browning, in Eliot and Pound, and to some extent in the poems I have discussed by Lowell and Berryman, the poem spoken by a character becomes, thereby, less a statement by the poet, and more a particular event. The same pursuit plays a role in the techniques sometimes referred to as "imagism"; it also plays a role, I believe, in motivating the evasively odd, inward, sassy, and oblique contemporary manner whose coolness makes the charged objects of imagism seem abstract, moralizing—even polemical—by comparison. Even the extraordinary refinement of so-called "free" verse can be seen as part of a flight from abstraction or recurrence, a pursuit of the status of a thing, a unique moment in time.[2] In this light, the extreme, paradox-mongering forms of the New Criticism were part of the Romantic or nominalist tradition because such ways of reading try to sever the poem from the simple act of abstract declaration. It is tempting to extend this judgment to more currently fashionable theories of poetics, according to which reading is an "all-but-impossible act, and if strong is always a misreading," and "there are *no* texts, but only relationships *between* texts."[3] These unpleasant, obscurantist critical contortions may stem partly from the same motives as the unutterably more attractive strategies devised by poets in their poems.

Strictly speaking, the ultimate goal of the nominalist poem is logically impossible. Language is absolutely abstract, a web of concepts and patterns; and if one believes experience to consist of unique, ungeneralizable moments, then the gap between language and experience is absolute. But the pursuit of the goal, or the effort to make the gap seem less than absolute, has produced some of the most remarkable and moving poetry in the language. Naturally, it has produced much dross, too. My proposition is that the difference between the dross and vulgarization on the one hand, and genuine work on the other, is a sense of cost, misgiving, difficulty.

That is, the peculiar, somewhat paradoxical project—to make an art's medium seem less what it is—produces brilliant techniques and new assumptions. Then, as generations pass, those techniques and assumptions come to seem the only way of writing. The original premises and difficulties of the style, and the original dilemma of mind, become obscured. This is what I mean by the expression "vulgarization":

> A poem should be wordless
> As the flight of birds

This chestnut, it will be recalled, also says:

> A poem should be motionless in time
> As the moon climbs

And concludes:

> A poem should be equal to:
> Not true
>
> For all the history of grief
> An empty doorway and a maple leaf
>
> For love
> The leaning grasses and two lights above the sea—
>
> A poem should not mean
> But be.[4]

One way of explaining why this familiar poem embarrasses the reader would be to point out, in detail, that a poem cannot be wordless; that sentences and rhythms move in time; that in order to be, the poem must mean . . . and so forth.

In response, however, this poem might be defended by the argument that its defective statements are figurative, not literal. Therefore, I suggest another way to object to the poem: it is corrupted by its bland, even smug attitude toward matters that have been defined as stressful moral and intellectual issues by Keats and many others. The poet mistakes the tense problem of the relationship between mind and the rest of nature for a kind of sweet credo or sentiment. (Any resemblance to the tone of Paul Verlaine's "Art *Poétique*" is superficial; where Verlaine's poem is arrogant and harsh, this one is intimate and satisfied.)

I may be guilty of critical overkill. On the other hand, the poem helps suggest where ideas go, and where they come back from. For one who at an early age encounters such a poem in a textbook,[5] there is perhaps no sense of loss in the proposition that a whole history of grief should be reduced to the pretty "open doorway and a maple leaf." The possibilities of poetry as a result become unconsciously fixed. They may seem not to include the "abstractions" of the elegy that begins:

Silence augmenteth grief, writing increaseth rage,

and includes the line:

Place, pensive, wails his fall whose presence was her pride.[6]

For Keats, the fancy cannot cheat us into believing that po-etry—or the mind itself—could exist without the quality embodied by these lines. The question is, how can that quality be used and modified as a means of approaching the opposite, yet somehow similar qualities of the nightingale. The nightingale is wordless, and compared to the poet and his work, it is motionless in time.

Poems in this tradition, then, take place between the conscious mind of which the poem is a part and the oblivious, natural universe toward which it yearns. The rest of this chapter will concentrate on a succession of modern and contemporary poems, poems that define widely varying aspects of that situation.

II. "Modern": "The Term," "The Most of It," and "The Snow Man"

The preceding discussion of Keats's "Ode" is meant to suggest a particular, somewhat cautious approach to certain familiar slogans of modernism: Williams's "No ideas but in things"; Stevens's "Not Ideas about the Thing but the Thing Itself"; or Pound's "Go in fear of abstractions" and "The proper and perfect symbol is the natural object." And there is Williams's famous red wheelbarrow, upon which "so much depends." These emblems and phrases, perhaps too often separated from their various contexts, suggest something like an extreme nominalist position. They suggest, in other words, an intellectual and poetic devotion to the utterly particular moment, the unique instant caught by the senses as in one flash of the retina.

But as I understand Keats, he tells us that to give oneself over utterly to the unreflecting "thing" is to become a sod. It is to die.

No matter what soft name we call that death, our imagination cannot, in the end, cheat us into believing that human nature can survive a flight from the solitude of consciousness, joining the rest of nature. The two kinds of death at stake in the "Ode," physical and intellectual, are finally one, because words and the human soul are both conceptual, they are both continuous projects in time. Words and the human soul both generalize, connecting moments of time, and organizing the particulars of experience.

What Keats does is to define the division between his conscious nature and the unconscious nature that surrounds him, building his definition with the conflicting emotions of longing and isolation. He states the problem in the most moving terms possible; that is also, I think, what much of the best modernist writing does. (As I have suggested in relation to "Ars Poetica," a hallmark of the worst writing is to underestimate the problem, or to deny it.)

Because this conflict, which strikes upon the very nature of language and poetry, has formed modernist rhetoric so completely, it sometimes seems hard to find a modern poem that does not touch on the problem at least glancingly, as a kind of second subject. Stevens could not write about war, without writing about this, too. But I want to take up some poems that make this conflict their central matter.

The emphasis, then, is less on the nature of "the image" or "the natural object" or "the thing itself" than on the nature of what perceives the thing. Or better, the emphasis is on the contrast between the two. That contrast is unmistakable even when it is kept more or less implicit:

The Term

A rumpled sheet
of brown paper
about the length

and apparent bulk
of a man was
rolling with the

wind slowly over
and over in
the street as

a car drove down
upon it and
crushed it to

the ground. Unlike
a man it rose
again rolling

with the wind over
and over to be as
it was before.

Williams suggests the abstract ideas that focus his poem by means of the title "The Term"; he tests those ideas, extending them to a kind of far point, by choosing an object whose poetic force is its insignificance.

The title taken with the poem suggests several kinds of "term." These meanings can be grouped under the two senses, "a term" meaning a set interval of time and "a term" meaning an expression for something else, ordinarily an expression in language. The theme of time and the theme of language, thus linked in an elegant wordplay, become welded by the poem itself, as they were welded by Keats in the "Ode to a Nightingale."

As to the terms of expression or language, the poem uses the term "a man" to describe its casual, drab bit of the physical world. As a term for the rumpled sheet of brown paper, "a man" evokes two attributes, and of these one is only "apparent." This word perhaps suggests that the terms the poet has found—or perhaps all terms?—are imperfect. This suggestion is confirmed by the transitional word that links the poem's two sentences:

> . . . and crushed it to

> the ground. Unlike
> a man. . . .

The two elements of the poem are "unlike." The effect as a whole is to remind us that all terms are by definition different from the things to which they refer. The terms of language are too human ("a man," "unlike a man"), and too grandly abstract, ever to capture the impenetrably casual, fragmented life of physical things. Close as the poet may seem to come, his poem consists of terms, not things.

(To a limited extent, the poem also invites us to consider the rolling, man-sized bit of rubbish as a "term" or metaphor for a man. However, to consider this meaning as anything but secondary tends to make the phrase "unlike a man" bathetic, a corny observation about mortality. This somewhat over-moralizing way of understanding the poem is as unsatisfying to

me as the other way of reading that declares that the poem is
"purely descriptive." Either reading would neglect the title and
the title's pursuance in the poem; but both mistakes become
more tempting if one ignores the tradition involved.)

As to the term or set interval of time, the poem makes us
aware that the period of attention to this street scene is arbi-
trary, and without inherent significance, by means of its final
phrase:

> Unlike
> a man it rose
> again rolling
>
> with the wind over
> and over to be as
> it was before.

That is, just as the object itself has no particular human mean-
ing, the period of time for which the poet chooses to watch it
has no particular human meaning. The brown paper and the
minute or so both become significant only because the poet
brings terms to them, or makes terms of them. By themselves,
they are boundless or "numberless" in the sense that neither the
paper nor the interval of time exists as a separate entity until a
mind declares it separate. I hope that this does not seem an idea
imposed on the poem; the phrase "over and over," coming when
it does, is striking evidence that the poem brings out certain
qualities that oblivious time has in common with the oblivious
physical world. Over and over, they are as they were before.
That is, consciousness does not touch or change them, and they
do not use terms. Like the nightingale of Keats or the buffalo in

Alan Stephens's poem, the moments that the poet chooses to isolate are not born for death. They cannot die because they are not continuous, distinct entities in time, in themselves. Only in the poem do they become terms, separate from the numberless continuum of nature.

(The secondary sense in which the phrase "unlike a man" does reflect upon human mortality, then, is a kind of philosophical corollary rather than a pointed "moral." Aware of time, the human mind alone cannot be as it was before, and so must experience the death of each moment—and, by extension, death itself.)

I hope that "The Term" presents a logical test or extreme case, in the sense that its apparently neutral, insignificant physical objects test the attraction of the inanimate thing. They also come closer than a natural landscape could come to presenting the physical world on its own terms—or so it could be argued. That is, the landscape or the bird does not know that it is beautiful or happy. "Beautiful" and "happy" are human terms, and by this argument Williams's car and windy street convey truly the anonymous blank, the stream of featureless particulars, which includes both street and landscape. On the other hand, this is a lovely scene: the peculiarly affecting blend of the drab and the beautiful achieved by this poem is also a human term, alien to unconscious "ease." Williams uses the terms of language and feeling to approach what is utterly unlike them; it is he who gives a beginning and an end to what passes by "over and over." The main point is that his poem does not disguise this cleavage between human words and the world, but rather struggles with it in order to set it before us.

Robert Frost's "The Most of It" provides a modern gloss on the aspect of Keats's poem suggested by the phrases "forlorn" and "sole self"—just as "The Term" may be seen as tracing the implications of "numberless," "immortal," and "a sod." But these remain sides of a single great theme, and in using the word "speech" Frost means something similar to "term":

> He thought he kept the universe alone;
> For all the voice in answer he could wake
> Was but the mocking echo of his own
> From some tree-hidden cliff across the lake.
> Some morning from the boulder-broken beach
> He would cry out on life, that what it wants
> Is not its own love back in copy speech,
> But counter-love, original response.
> And nothing ever came of what he cried
> Unless it was the embodiment that crashed
> In the cliff's talus on the other side,
> And then in the far distant water splashed.
> But after a time allowed for it to swim,
> Instead of proving human when it neared
> And someone else additional to him,
> As a great buck it powerfully appeared,
> Pushing the crumpled water up ahead,
> And landed pouring like a waterfall,
> And stumbled through the rocks with horny tread,
> And forced the underbrush—and that was all.

I hope that much of the relevance of this poem to what has been said so far in this chapter is apparent. The protagonist can find no voice or speech or terms of "keeping" in the universe but his own, human ones. Like Keats, when he sees or admires the landscape, he becomes aware that the concepts or words that he perceives with, his human terms and modes of perception, make him utterly unlike the landscape, which uses absolutely no terms of its own. He craves the logical verbal paradox of "original response": something that will spring from sources totally unlike him, yet somehow speak to him. The implication of that paradoxical phrase—that there is no solution, that the gulf is absolute—is strengthened by the emergence of the indifferent deer, which fades like Keats's nightingale into the dim underbrush.

I want to point out the language of diffidence, uncertainty, and depreciation—"He thought," "all the voice," "was but," "some . . . cliff," "some morning," "nothing ever came," "unless it was." It is also important that this diffident or minimizing element leaves the poem almost entirely at a point marked by the appearance of the buck, recurring only with the last three words of the poem. This diffident quality becomes almost embarrassed-sounding in the awkward charm of "copy speech" and other idiosyncratic, personality-ridden phrases. These too more or less vanish during the impressive description of the buck.

The poem, then, is on the theme that we can never see nature in its own terms, but only in our own. The emotion in response to that is loneliness, for the more beautiful and impressive the scene is, the more separate and nonhuman it is. Its attributes are evoked by the forcefully inflected verbs of the description:

> As a great buck it powerfully appeared,
> Pushing the crumpled water up ahead,
> And landed pouring like a waterfall,
> And stumbled through the rocks with horny tread,
> And forced the underbrush—and that was all.

It is indifferent, powerful, beautiful, unaware, and its parts fade into one another. Its callous tread is hard, formidable, and separate.

The subject of the verbs is "it," and the reference of that pro-
noun is to the word "embodiment." This peculiar word, which
thus dominates the poem's grammatical structure, occurs in the
line of greatest rhythmical violence, and on the boundary be-
tween the diffident, idiosyncratic diction and the more pure
and stern diction of the description.

"Embodiment" is a peculiar word in at least two ways. First,
it looks like an "abstract" rather than a "concrete" word; but its
root is the most "concrete" of words, and its meaning entails the
making-physical of something abstract. Second, the word seems
to raise an unanswerable question: what does this terrifically
naturalistic animal "embody"?

Thus, the word raises the nominalist-realist question of
words and things, first by its own nature, and then by what it
denotes. The only answer to the question, "embodiment of
what?" is that the swimming buck embodies ease—or the qual-
ity of embodying nothing. He embodies pure being, without
abstract referent, and, since that purity or ease is the attribute
of all undifferentiated nature, he also embodies the whole land-
scape—just as any other part of it would: bush, droplet, night-
ingale, or shadow.

By embodying the absence of conceptual meaning, the buck
is meaningless or literally insignificant; but since that insignifi-
cance characterizes the whole natural universe, the buck is also
the embodiment of something immense. Therefore, both senses
of the final phrase—"and that was all"—take force. Like the
nightingale, the buck is a series of details—and that is all. But
because those details fade into the rest of the mute universe, he
is also as good a representative as any of All.

Two aspects of the poem are significant in relation to
contemporary poetry. First, though the buck is literally

"insignificant," his unaware dignity is enormous, and it is the poet's voice, thrown back on itself, which trails off into the self-conscious depreciation of "that was all." The individual personality, the small voice with its ironically awkward logisms ("counterlove," "someone else additional to him") becomes a way of recognizing metaphysical circumstance.

In a word, one is forlorn. And there are graceful ways to indicate that feeling, more or less. Frank O'Hara's poem "Dialogues" opens with the line:

You find me tentative and frivolous, don't you?

and concludes with this deliberately, diffidently flattened language:

And there comes a dawn for you, too, comes one
like spring, like water in spring and merry birds,
where the heart feels openly as the eye sees,
ultimate peace, an instant of this world's bloody love.

This is the sole self expressing a sort of decent irony about its own uniqueness, "keeping" the patterns and memories of the universe while experience passes in one perfectly whole "instant" after another.

A second way in which "The Most of It" pertains to later writing depends upon the somewhat threatening, perhaps violent—or "perilous"—aspect of the powerful, crashing, and callous animal. Because the un-keeping, numberless natural universe seems to invite the mind to die, and because it is alien, nature is sometimes seen as inimical, full of spiritual danger. This aspect of the tradition has been described (for instance) by Robert Langbaum and by Bernard Bergonzi.[7] In pulling away from the temptation to seem or to be "already with thee," the sole self defends itself.

Here are examples from two enormously different poets; first, the opening stanza of Yvor Winters's poem on the story of Gawaine and the Green Knight:

> Reptilian green the wrinkled throat,
> Green as a bough of yew the beard;
> He bent his head, and so I smote;
> Then for a thought my vision cleared.

The protagonist is tested by the Green Knight's lady, who "like a forest vine,/ Grew in my arms":

> Her beauty, lithe, unholy, pure,
> Took shapes that I had never known;
> And had I once been insecure,
> Had grafted laurel in my bone.

The Knight "let me go with what I knew," and the poem closes:

> I left the green bark and the shade,
> Where growth was rapid, thick, and still;
> I found a road that men had made
> And rested on a drying hill.

This, with its explicit "road that men had made," is perhaps unusually moralistic, or unusually fearful of the power and attraction in unconscious nature. Yet the encounter is valued for "what I knew" or learned. And in even the most enthusiastically "Romantic" and nature-loving of contemporary poets it is possible to find something of this fear or unease:

Piute Creek

One granite ridge
A tree, would be enough
Or even a rock, a small creek,
A bark shred in a pool.
Hill beyond hill, folded and twisted
Tough trees crammed
In thin stone fractures
A huge moon on it all, is too much.
The mind wanders. A million
Summers, night air still and the rocks
Warm. Sky over endless mountains.
All the junk that goes with being human
Drops away, hard rock wavers
Even the heavy present seems to fail
This bubble of a heart.
Words and books
Like a small creek off a high ledge
Gone in the dry air.

A clear, attentive mind
Has no meaning but that
Which sees is truly seen.
No one loves rock, yet we are here.
Night chills. A flick
In the moonlight
Slips into Juniper shadow:
Back there unseen
Cold proud eyes
Of Cougar or Coyote
Watch me rise and go.

This poem by Gary Snyder manages to be at once frank and uneasy, about seeing and being seen, dealing in its wobbling yet persistent way with "mind" on the one hand and the vast dry expanse of rock on the other. Books, words, and the condition of being human seem to be described frankly as junk, with a whole-hearted anti-intellectualism; on the other hand, the mind's grasp on the present moment in the frame of time is associated uneasily with life and death, this "bubble of a heart." The poem suggests an uneasy desire to qualify its feelings in a way that the language of the poem cannot quite solve.

It is as though Snyder is tempted to call the gorgeous, too vast and stony blank of the night by sweet names, but finds that he cannot quite do it. "Night chills." And insofar as it is animated or inhabited, the landscape watches the human creature leave. That watching is not merely less than loving; it seems to exclude the departing human, with alert impassivity. Though the capitals of "Cougar or Coyote" suggest a tentative effort to mythologize the animal, it remains perfectly alien, as well as unseen and unidentified. The particularity implied by the capitalization into proper nouns is only an idea of the poet's. Like the nightingale, the animal itself is not seen, but remains a continuous part of the dim landscape.

It might be said that "Piute Creek" is merely uncertain and confused, while "The Most of It" hauntingly and precisely gives shape to uncertainty and confusion—just as some readers will find Winters's "Sir Gawaine and the Green Knight" too stiffly explicit, compared with Frost's poem. The point is that, for all of these poets, something unaware and self-enclosed in nature, something that they feel drawn to be with, leads them to realms perilous and forlorn.

Wallace Stevens's great poem "The Snow Man" is more ambitious intellectually, in relation to the matters I have been tracing, than "The Term" or "The Most of It."

If "The Term" illustrates the recurrence of ideas emblemized here by Keats's phrases "numberless," "immortal" and "a sod," while "The Most of It" illustrates related themes that I have associated with the words "forlorn," "sole" and "perilous," then in "The Snow Man" Stevens concentrates on those aspects of this one theme that concern the fancy, and how well it can or cannot cheat. (And also, the man made of snow is a special example of the earthen sod, and Stevens's "one" is a sole self . . . but this verbal device has served its purpose.)

The poem's rhythm, elegant and nearly hypnotic, helps to unify the vivid physical details with the intricately abstract propositions of the sentences:

> One must have a mind of winter
> To regard the frost and the boughs
> Of the pine trees crusted with snow;
>
> And have been cold a long time
> To behold the junipers shagged with ice,
> The spruces rough in the distant glitter
>
> Of the January sun; and not to think
> Of any misery in the sound of the wind,
> In the sound of a few leaves,
>
> Which is the sound of the land
> Full of the same wind
> That is blowing in the same bare place

For the listener, who listens in the snow,
And, nothing himself, beholds
Nothing that is not there and the nothing that is.

The poem is well known, and the reader will be able to formulate for himself most of what I might say about it in relation to the themes of this chapter.

To summarize, the poem meditates the theoretical possibility of seeing nature purely, on its own termless terms: no "happiness" in which to be happy; no "like a man" or "unlike a man"; no deluded expectation of anything like "speech" or "love" counter to one's own—just the distinct phenomena that compose a winter landscape, and that is all.

One would need a mind enormously purified of human responses, in order to feel that way—figuratively speaking, a cold or wintry mind. But in order to remind us that winter's "misery" is only in the observing mind, like the nightingale's "happiness," Stevens first irresistibly evokes that illusion of misery in the wind—an illusion of which one *must* at least "think," before dismissing it, unless one's mind is literally cold: dead, or an inert ball molded from the snow of winter.

In other words, only an imaginary, supremely cold-minded witness could completely avoid anthropomorphizing the bitter winter scene, avoid seeing it in human terms. In order to see that beautiful, indifferent scene as purely as possible, Stevens encourages us to imagine that theoretical witness—the way he encourages us to see the landscape as harsh or miserable, as part of realizing that it is neither, but purely itself. (Even the literal, physical truth that the wind's sound is the sound of the land becomes full of mysterious human feeling—because of the nature of human language, the poet demonstrates.)

That theoretical observer, oddly, has an actual representation in the snow man. Anthropomorphic snow, somewhat comic with Stevens's peculiarly elegant and Romantic comedy, the snow man embodies the theoretically ideal observer who commits no "pathetic fallacy" while beholding the landscape. ("Beholds" is a brilliant word for what the inert creature does.)

To reach that condition, seeing the physical world only for what it is—being "at one" with it—and knowing it fully as nothing *to* any person, one would have to cease existing. Perfect immersion in the thing itself is a kind of stony death. The living mind is not so completely "of" winter that it can keep from thinking of misery a little, or of happiness or some other affect.

This brings us full circle, back to the "Ode to a Nightingale" and the nothingness that is so attractive that the fancy half-cheats one into calling it sweet names. In Keats's poem, to think of oneself as "already with thee" through the fairy tale of sweet names is to destroy the poor, dull brain and die,

> To thy high requiem become a sod.

That is, to become nothing.

In Stevens's poem, to imagine a human being who can see natural things purely in themselves, one must imagine a man-shaped cypher,

> who listens in the snow,
> And, nothing himself, beholds
> Nothing that is not there and the nothing that is.

Absolute freedom from illusion is as remote from the possibilities of life as absolute embrace of illusion ("already with thee"). In fact, the two are remarkably similar. Like Keats's "sod" the snow man's situation may be, on some terrible level, what one desires, or what is most viable philosophically. But both of those far points are inconsistent with ongoing life, and human life's dull baggage of perplexing terms, words, and forms, the means we use to "keep" the universe in time. Whatever is there, in the landscape—pure of our speech and concepts, our "happiness" or "misery" or "like a man"—it is nothing to us. We cannot see it pure of such terms; we cannot see its aloof beauty, except in those terms.

III. Generalities

The poetic subject I have been discussing may seem rarefied, removed from the doings of life. What about poems concerned with such matters as making love or eating a banana, about war, politics, or family life? One response to such a question is that the poems just discussed deal by implication with the subject of death, and with the even more grandly general subject of contingency in time. Those concerns govern and color other experiences—including war, politics, making love, and so forth.

Our way of writing a dramatic poem, of alluding to history, of dealing with ideas while composing a poem, of setting up a discursive passage—of making choices even as to rhythm and punctuation—are all colored by a cautious or skeptical approach toward language and its abstract nature. The act of discourse and the act of poetry have become so intricately, or even tenuously, connected, that the nature of their connection has become an implied or direct theme of poetry.

In contemporary poetry, some of the frequently encountered responses to this theme might be ranged under three loose headings—meant to be suggestive, rather than exhaustive or rigid.

(1) A "naive" or (so to speak) "pre-Keats"[8] insistence that the poet is somehow "already with thee" or, unlike Frost's protagonist, has received an apprehensible, loving response from the unconscious world. Just as Keats, at the roots of the tradition, might be called post-Romantic to the extent that we call the fourth stanza of his poem "Romantic," so Roethke, in the lines I have quoted earlier, might be considered a naive predecessor of Keats. I am also thinking of more diverse phenomena, such as Denise Levertov on the toilet seat exclaiming "the authentic!" or Robert Bly, simply flattening or "simplifying" the diction of Keats:

> And swim in the sea,
> Not always walking on dry land,
> And, dancing, find in the trees a saviour,
> A home in dark grass,
> And nourishment in death.

("A HOME IN DARK GRASS")

The "Ode to a Nightingale" and the three modern poems by Williams, Frost, and Stevens are high points of conscious detachment from this love of death and unconsciousness: a high point of judging that love. One could call such moments a part of the post-Romantic tradition within the ongoing persistence of Romanticism.

Comedy, wit, slapstick, irony—as in the Levertov example or in Allen Ginsberg's appealing line,

> You were never no locomotive, Sunflower, you were a
> sunflower!

do not make the feeling any less sincerely envying or admiring toward the utterly particular, unreflecting instant, or any less dissatisfied with concepts and terms.

Similarly, I would include under this heading writing that is sensational—that is, literally, writing that emphasizes particular physical sensations or circumstances. The single sensation is the unit, the reality of nominalist experience. At its best, such work matches the mysteriously touching accuracy of Williams—Elizabeth Bishop's "Filling Station" is such a poem, I think, as quotation should be enough to show. Here are a few stanzas from the middle, to suggest the whole poem and the thousand poems by lesser hands that fail at such projects:

> Father wears a dirty,
> oil-soaked monkey suit
> that cuts him under the arms,
> and several quick and saucy
> and greasy sons assist him
> (it's a family filling station),
> all quite thoroughly dirty.
>
> Do they live in the station?
> It has a cement porch
> behind the pumps, and on it

a set of crushed and grease-
impregnated wickerwork;
on the wicker sofa
a dirty dog, quite comfy.

Some comic books provide
the only note of color—
of certain color. They lie
upon a big dim doily
draping a taboret
(part of the set), beside
a big hirsute begonia.

Here, the poet creates the illusion, largely with feel for idiom, that sensory perception *is* meaning. The nature of the life observed, and even the nature of the speaker's life—totally different, not unadmiring—are developed through what seems, on the surface, to be merely a physical and idiomatic precision.

Yet we are in effect told about a kind of drawn contest between the meticulous vigor of the writer and the sloppy vigor of the family, both poet and grease-monkeys "filling" the potential dull blank of one space and time, filling it with an unexpected, crazy, deceptively off-hand kind of elegance or ornament.

Bishop conveys such moral and emotional judgments as though they were merely reported by a neutral informant, an informant who relies largely upon that relatively naive device, the adjective. The "dirty" that begins and ends the first stanza seems so direct and, so to speak, honest, that we hardly notice the thorough way in which the other modifiers in the stanza convey their complex enthusiasm, amusement, tempered condescension. Adjectives, according to a sound rule of thumb for writing classes, do not make "good descriptions." By writing almost as though she were too plain and straightforward to have heard of such a rule, Bishop loads characterizations of herself and her subject into the "comfy" dog, the "dim" doily, the "hirsute" begonia; the quietest possible virtuoso strokes. In such ways, the separate sensations of the eye are made to seem identical with the verbal "observations."

In contrast, when a poet proceeds as though such illusions were not the final products of art, but the principles of art, starting points—then the result is precious, self-consciously and elaborately "direct." The kind of writing I mean seems to have taken the "naive" neutrality, which Bishop works up as a shrewd illusion, for its actual method. Again, I think that quotation serves to illustrate the difference:

> I am driving; it is dusk; Minnesota.
> The stubble field catches the last growth of sun.
> The soybeans are breathing on all sides.
> Old men are sitting before their houses on carseats
> In the small towns. I am happy,
> The moon rising above the turkey sheds.[9]

This drifts from uncertainty into boastfulness, a kind of more-imagistic-than-thou attitude. Moreover, "growth," "breathing" and the generic plural of "old men" are unlikely and "poetic"— more for tone than for information. If Bishop tells us surprisingly much in a quiet voice resembling speech, these lines about the dusk, the moon, and the soybeans tell us surprisingly little in a voice of mysterious, bardic hush.

While I am being somewhat negative or surly, I will propose that there is a still more abusive way of writing within this "sensational" category: when the adjective "sensational" applies in a couple of senses, and the poet grabs our presumably sleepy interest with the startling or the bizarre: a cynical version of the nominalist poem. The poem of the woman's thoughts as she falls to earth from an airliner, insofar as it is held together by anecdotal interest, fails: it becomes merely flamboyant testimony for the poet's lively imagination.

(2) Another, contrasting category consists of refinements and extensions of the work done by poets like Stevens and Frost, exploring the relation between the isolated, conscious mind and its continuous, unreflecting habitat. This is the work that more or less consciously undertakes the central issues and applies to them the strategies and techniques of modernism. This category pretty much coincides with the material dealt with in the next, final section of this chapter. At this point, I will try to use two enormously different poets to suggest the range of such "mainstream" work, a range vast in quality, manner, approach.

That large, various terrain may be suggested by mentioning the exquisite, perhaps impenetrably dark epistemological poems of Alvin Feinman, and in contrast John Ashbery's systematic, oddly destructive assemblages of "pure" words and forms of speech, beautifully fashioned and isolated from all but the ghost of an apprehensible physical world.

The contrast of styles is instructive; first, Feinman gravely articulating the vacuum or the longing between himself and the natural scene that dazzles him practically into incomprehensibility:

Something, something, the heart here
Misses, something it knows it needs
Unable to bless—the wind passes;
A swifter shadow sweeps the reeds,
The heart a colder contrast brushes.

So this fool, face-forward, belly
Pressed among the rushes, plays out
His pulse to the dune's long slant
Down from blue to bluer element,
The bold encompassing drink of air

And namelessness, a length compound
Of want and oneness the shore's mumbling
Distantly tells—something a wing's
Dry pivot stresses, carved
Through barrens of stillness and glare:

The naked close of light in light,
Light's spare embrace of blade and tremor
Stealing the generous eye's plunder
Like a breathing banished from the lung's
Fever, lost in parenthetic air.

("PILGRIM HEIGHTS")

Those lines (the first four of seven stanzas) constitute a sentence
in verse that is elegant yet intense and even heated. But despite
moments like the phrase "this fool," the tone is remarkably im-
personal; most of all, the poem often slips into darkness.

Ashbery's manner is cool and elegant. He does not slip into
darkness; he takes darkness for granted and speaks from it,

language somewhat analogous at times to paint in a nonrepresentational picture:

> There is no remedy for this "packaging" which has
>   supplanted the old sensations.
> Formerly there would have been architectural screens
>   at the point where the action became most difficult
> As a path trails off into shrubbery—confusing,
>   forgotten, yet continuing to exist.
> But today there is no point in looking to imaginative
>   new methods
> Since all of them are in constant use. The most that
>   can be said for them further
> Is that erosion produces a kind of dust or exaggerated
>   pumice
> Which fills space and transforms it, becoming a medium
> In which it is possible to recognize oneself.

("DEFINITION OF BLUE")

It could be said of Feinman's style, in the first quotation, that it is terribly "abstract": the emotion could not survive an approach any more strictly limited to the mind encountering the senses; the conceptual theme is not compromised a whit. It is like reading Hart Crane without even the vague, heroic myths. No sense of an individual human character, or circumstance, qualifies the philosophical issues raised by the instance of a generalized man in the landscape.

Ashbery's style is "abstract" in quite another way; the language comes closer than one might have thought possible to being, itself, a nominalistic particular: pure, referring to nothing else, unique. The drawback or danger of this kind of "abstraction" lies in the requisite air of irony or put-on, more or less extreme reservations hedging the ideas referred to by the words: and the less serious the ideas, the less serious the emotion. Thus, the note of positive belief at the end of "Definition of Blue" fails to work as well as the more puckish passage quoted above:

> And yet it results in a downward motion, or rather a
>   floating one
> In which the blue surroundings drift slowly up and
>   past you
> To realize themselves some day, while you, in this
>   nether world that could not be better
> Waken each morning to the exact value of what you
>   did and said, which remains.

The ideal here is, perhaps, the goal of pure, nominalistic perception: each fact, action, and act of word, almost as if undistorted by ideas. Or, it may be some other "exact value." In either case, it fails to convince, because the "abstract" style on which the poem builds is too funny—

> The rise of capitalism parallels the advance of
>   romanticism
> And the individual is dominant until the close of the
>   nineteenth century.
> In our own time, mass practices have sought to
>   submerge the personality
> By ignoring it, which has caused it instead to branch
>   out in all directions

> Far from the permanent tug that used to be its notion
> of "home."
>
> ("DEFINITION OF BLUE," OPENING LINES)

—too successfully funny in its daft skepticism for us to take any subsequent idea quite seriously. Oddly enough, Feinman's more "impersonal," perhaps arid manner expresses an emotionally richer kind of abstraction. This seems odd because, to the extent that "Definition of Blue" appears to destroy happily the meanings and referents of language, it must supply interest by means of charm, comedy, and personality—at which point this heading or category shades off into the next one.

In summary, I have tried to find two extremes of a kind; if Feinman's problem is a clotted obscurity, the problem of Ashbery's artfully "destroyed" language is the reader's potential boredom with the virtual absence of denotation. The boredom must be held off (and is) with an expert play of surprises, gags, and daffy charm. Such play offers a way to avoid, on the one hand, Feinman's cerebral, ecstatic kind of landscape poem, and on the other hand a dated, sentimental "imagism": the "single raindrop" of the Iowa *haiku*, the snowflake in the horse's mane. Those solemn clichés share Romantic roots with Feinman, and with the sophisticated antics of Ashbery or O'Hara. Disparate as the styles may seem, they are attempts to solve the same, central dilemma.

(3) The "surrealist" or playful putting forward of the poet's personality deserves a category of its own. The poems I have in mind here will be dealt with again, more than once, in this book; the purpose at this point is to relate such writing to the

tradition I have associated with Keats, Stevens, and others. That can be done by explaining my reservations about the term "surrealism" as applied to certain recent poems, and by showing why the "surrealist" and the playful, or jackanapes, strains go together.

If the surrealism of Breton's manifestoes is playful, it is so in the most anarchic, literally revolutionary way. In any case, historical surrealism, as I understand it, was deeply allied with ideas about dreams, Freudian and otherwise, and also with related ideas concerning a profound cultural unconscious. The word "profound," a mining of unexplored depths, seems appropriate: a stating of mysterious connections and unacknowledged junctures, a reality beyond ordinary reality, richer in meaning and emotion.

That warm, somewhat soupy idea seems to me quite irrelevant to much of the "surrealist" poetry of the late sixties and the seventies. As I will try to show, later, by quotation, the contemporary variety is not warm, but cool; it is a matter of dazzling, elegantly manifold surfaces, rather than depths: wild event or anecdote, rather than dream; inchoate, self-enclosed events rather than disclosed junctures; above all, a daffy or sinister absurdity in this one reality, rather than a more profound realm beyond. The young poet who writes a poem about hurling 78-rpm records at Holstein cows[10] is not thinking of a deeper dream-reality behind ordinary life; he is denying the distinction. Or, consider Mark Strand's charming poem "Courtship," which begins:

> There is a girl you like so you tell her
> your penis is big, but that you cannot get yourself
> to use it. Its demands are ridiculous, you say,

even self-defeating, but to be honored somehow,
briefly, inconspicuously in the dark.

When she closes her eyes in horror,
    you take it all back. You tell her you're almost
a girl yourself and can understand why she is shocked.
When she is about to walk away, you tell her
    you have no penis, that you don't

know what got into you. You get on your knees.
She suddenly bends down to kiss your shoulder and
    you know
you're on the right track. You tell her you want
to bear children and that is why you seem confused. . . .

This is not Breton's pistol at the head of all ordinary values, but
a nearly sweet, interior form of social comedy.

The new surrealism merges with the style of put-on and egre-
gious personality because of the motive to avoid abstract state-
ment or, at least, to avoid unqualified commitment to such
statement. On the one hand, there is the diction I will come to
in my last chapter, associated most, perhaps, with W. S. Mer-
win: "silence" and "light" and "water" and "breath" (as of the
soybeans a few pages above), flowing, particulate substances,
shapeless and pure and, most of all, tacit. On the other hand,
there is a personality: evasive, a bit fey, sexy, nutty in an Ameri-
can's kidding way, and elaborately unaffected—somewhat like
the personality of those self-describedly "crazy" high-school
kids and "wild" fraternity boys of the sane, tame late fifties,
some of whom are today's young poets.

Though European and Latin American comparisons are
sometimes adduced, this particular style of deadpan fantasy is

at least as close to the freewheeling unreason and personal downrightness of "Oh Susannah" or of Twain's "Missing White Elephant." In support of that generalization, and to suggest other roots for the manner, I will quote a whole poem by Russell Edson:

A Performance at Hog Theater

There was once a hog theater
where hogs performed as men might
had men been hogs.

One hog said
I will be a hog in a field which has found a mouse
which is being eaten by the same hog
which is in the field
and which has found the mouse;
which I am performing as my contribution
to the performer's art.

Oh let's just be hogs, cried an old hog.

And so the hogs streamed out of the theater crying,
only hogs, only
hogs . . .

Now, this is nothing quite so direct as parody; but those relative pronouns, and the cadence, recall an austere performance, a testing of impossibly high and artificial standards, in sonorous terms:

Which is the sound of the land
Full of the same wind
That is blowing in the same bare place

For the listener who listens in the snow,
And, nothing himself, beholds
Nothing that is not there and the nothing that is.

An analogy for the relation between these two poems might be
the way that Lewis Carroll exorcizes the attraction of Words-
worth's "Resolution and Independence" with the White
Knight's poem—

And now, if e'er by chance I put
My fingers into glue,
Or madly squeeze a right-hand foot
Into a left-hand shoe,
Or if I drop upon my toe
A very heavy weight,
I weep, for it reminds me so
Of that old man I used to know.

Edson's poem, like the White Knight's, deflates a grandiloquent
evocation of bare, wintry simplicity with "genuine" simplicity,
a simplicity that emphasizes the local, the natural, and the
irresponsible.

(The analogy with Carroll tempts one to compare the col-
loquial, clever, sophisticated, mock-innocent, whimsical man-
ners of some contemporary poets with Carroll, Lear, Belloc,
Chesterton, the cult of irresponsibility among those successors
to the Romantics: the rolling English drunkard, for example,
who made the rolling English road of Chesterton's poem, nearly
seems a contemporary protagonist, or perhaps a Victorian
great-uncle of Kenneth Koch.)

To look at it another way, the surrealist-jackanapes style
avoids the magisterial tone, and the philosophical approach, of

Stevens, while dealing with a subject much like his: the place of human imagination in a world unlike itself. Similar as the material may be, it is approached so that it seems not to be an elaborate performance; the air of performance is dispelled by a technique perhaps first perfected by Allen Ginsberg, with his

> America I'm putting my queer shoulder to the wheel
>
> ("AMERICA")

or

> What thoughts I have of you tonight, Walt Whitman, for
> I walked down the sidestreets under the trees with a
> headache self-conscious looking at the full moon.
>
> ("A SUPERMARKET IN CALIFORNIA")

This vigorous comedy of the self can be adapted[11] so as to avoid making a big deal (as one of the poets in question might say) of the individual and his imagination.

But traditions persist, and not only negatively. For instance, Stevens has a comedy of his own, more auditory and less personal. He is always prepared to mock himself urbanely for making a religion of the imagination and its disciplines, even during the very rites themselves. In "Bantam in Pine Woods" Chieftain Iffucan, in caftan of tan, struts with a gaudy, vulnerable appeal no less clownish and profound than James Tate's "Blue Booby," who lives

> on the bare rocks
> of Galapagos
> and fears nothing.

Part baboon and part ideal poet, the male Boobies
                    do not
          make fools of themselves
          chasing after the young
          ladies. Rather,
          they gather the blue
          objects of the world
          and construct from them

          a nest.

Such utterances, raffish and hieratic, are not far from the grave
intellectual play of Stevens.

I am not speaking of influence—the idea is not that all of
these poets are Stevens-readers trying to remove the chieftain's
markings. Rather, they are writing so as to avoid a grand rheto-
ric and a priestly view of the imagination that, I think, reach
their height in Stevens's work. The persistence of a traditional
theme and circumstance makes that rhetoric and that elevated
view appeal strongly, so strongly that they must be avoided—
and even, as in Edson's poem, punished.

Nor is the conclusion necessarily that traditions dilute in
time. It might seem that young poets imitating older practitio-
ners of the style at hand (such as O'Hara or Kenneth Koch) are
struggling, at best, to see which one of them will get to stand in
relation to Stevens as Cowley stands to Donne. But, in fact,
such matters—the question of how great or small work will
turn out to be—depend upon the imponderable attributes of
talent and genius. It is only possible to study the seeming risks
and opportunities.

Having said that, I feel free to mention such a risk—or is it
an opportunity in disguise? The "surreal" and "put-on" or gag-

style aspects of the manner can shift in confusing ways. Mark Strand has written beautiful lines, and inventively funny ones. But which response is called for, or how are they mingled, in these lines, which begin his poem "Inside the Story"?:

> He never spoke much
> but he began to speak even less.

On the one hand, the reticence that has been my subject is summarized. But the reader may wonder nervously if this is or is not deliberate self-parody. Is he—or *isn't* he?—kidding?

IV. "Contemporary"

I have tried to outline the persistence, in modern and contemporary poems, of certain Romantic ideas and expectations. These recurring concepts have been well described by many writers on nineteenth- and twentieth-century poetry, in various fruitful ways. For present purposes, the most helpful terms have to do with words and things, and the problematical relation between them, which is the relation between forms and events: at times, between ourselves and the happenings of life, our souls and our sensations.

The quotation marks bracketing "Romantic," "Modern," and "Contemporary" indicate (in part) this same idea: that the problematical relation between words and things does not change, from one time to another, however much stylistic responses to the dilemma may vary. The circumstance or philosophical situation remains essentially the same. And perhaps even the range of emotional responses to the subject has not varied much, either—though the stylistic responses have varied enormously.

Within such general terms, particular poems and their strange ways may turn out to deserve the description "traditional." *The Paris Review* in 1972 published, in the center of a page headed by the author's name, the following untitled poem by Bruce Andrews:[12]

Bananas are an example.

Even among poems four words long, this one might seem inscrutable, unyielding. However, it is traditional, even literary in theme. (This is true apart from the poem's conservative technique; viz., it is a complete declarative sentence with predicate copula, the sentence is marked by initial capital letter and terminal period, the abstract expression "example" elucidates the concrete reference "banana," and so forth.)

The poem is about exemplifying; and to exemplify is to make a connection between the realm of things and the realm of ideas, yoking thought and experience by a gesture of the will. The same linking action stands behind the word "embodiment" at the fulcrum of Frost's "The Most of It." Williams supplies a more likely association for most readers, with the highly specified, rain-glazed item of farm equipment; upon that instance— or example?—of reality, "so much"—including much literary study—"depends." Even the nightingale is one arbitrary example of nature's continuous presence.

Comic and reductive, Andrews's poem calls attention to the somewhat arbitrary nature of any connection between specific examples and general ideas. Bananas are an example of yellow things, of fruits, of natural objects, of poetic images. They constitute a suitable example of the prosaic (have one?), the exotic (where do they grow?), the political (who picks them?), the sexual (are they not phallic?). In short, like other examples, bananas might be taken as a specific instance of an infinite number of categories. They might be made to exemplify nearly anything.[13]

Which is to say, they do not *particularly* exemplify anything; none of that infinite number of categories commands an inherent, necessary connection to bananas. Even "food" or "edible fruit" must be "made to" belong with the particular instance, for like other connections these are "made" by the mind. The reductive comedy makes a point that is not only traditional, but literary: bananas are an example of "imagery" or "symbols" too. From the nominalist tradition of skepticism about language and poetry, it is a small step to find language and poetry absurd or ridiculous.

Moreover, since the poem declares that bananas *are,* after all, an example, the poem leans a little toward the conservative or philosophical-realist side of the problem; arbitrary or silly as it may be to choose one connection from an infinity, the connection is there.

A word, at this somewhat bizarre point, about the plural noun, in predicate with the singular article: "Bananas" is an example of a word that refers to a concrete reality. But the word itself is a general category and not a single concrete experience, as its plural form emphasizes. Because "bananas" is a generality, divorced from any particular experience, the poem does not specify physical reality (the glaze of rainwater, the pale, pithy strips of moist inner peel) any more than it specifies the idea exemplified.

So, bananas are an example of particulars, but "bananas" is an example of an abstraction.

But I sense the reader dozing. Is this a poem? Is it a good poem? The poem itself does not apparently try to undertake the terms of those questions. The writer borrows a manner readily available and treats a theme similarly available, so that the skill and the feeling both come as much from a tradition as from an individual. In a sense, there is no author (though there indubitably is an actual "Bruce Andrews").

The not-trying, then, need not be thought of as essentially—or only—prankish. The effacement of the poet himself, as he becomes his tradition, recalls analogous writing of other periods, as when the Early Tudor poet Henry Parker, Lord Morley writes to his posterity sixteen lines to be written over a chamber door where he was wont to lie at Hallingbury, expressing himself by expressing traditional ideas in a traditional way:

> But always I thought to bring the mind to rest,
> And that thought of all thoughts I judge it the best.

As with the banana-poem, the manner and the paraphrasable proposition—and even, perhaps, the feeling—waited ready to hand before the poet wrote the poem. The matter or sentiment in both cases is presented with the absolute minimum of variation, and the manner or style, in both cases, pretends to no innovation. One's response to the question of how "good" such writing is will depend first of all upon one's response to the tradition voiced.

Certainly, the two traditions could not be more different. Lord Morley invites us to use what he calls the "gentle art" of abstract reasoning in order to arrive at the idea and feeling of peace. The banana-poem toys with the possibility that one might think only of a particular experience, and not at all of the categories that it exemplifies—which for Lord Morley might mean not to think at all.

Well; the one thing harder for Morley to imagine than the untitled poem about examples might be my pages about that poem. I have tried to show (a) how a crazy-looking poem can be extremely traditional, in the sense that its manner and matter can be understood only through their historical background, and (b) an example of the nominalist dilemma reduced to a kind of Absolute Zero.

More considerable poems have dealt with that dilemma—a philosophical problem that is also, particularly for a poet, a personal problem, however it is formulated—and dealt with it in a fairly direct way. The poet patiently works out the relation between particular realities and general perceptions in himself and his art. One such poem is Charles Tomlinson's "Reflections":

> Like liquid shadows. The ice is thin
> 　Whose mirror smears them as it intercepts
> Withdrawing colors; and where the crust,
> 　As if a skin livid with tautening scars,
> Whitens, cracks, it steals from these deformations
> 　A style too tenuous for the image. A mirror lies, and
> Flawed like this, may even lie with art,
> 　With reticence: "I exaggerate nothing,
> For the reflections—scarcely half you see—
> 　Tell nothing of what you feel." Nature is blind
> Like habit. Distrust them. We, since no mirrors,
> 　Are free both to question this deployment

And to arrange it—what we reflect
  Being what we choose. Though without deference,
We are grateful. When we perceive, as keen
  As the bridge itself, a bridge inlaying the darkness
Of smooth water, our delight acknowledges our debt—
  To nature, from whom we choose;
And, fencing that fullness back, to habit,
  The unsheathed image piercing our winter sleep.

Reflections are thoughts, consciousness considering itself; and, reflections (as in a mirror) are objects. The two senses merge in several ways, notably because physical reflections, shadowy objects in themselves, present or suggest, as ghost-versions or references, other more solid objects. So that the ice or smooth water, in relation to the bridge or to the colors of the world, not only transforms but also in a way refers; similar in those ways to the mind, it produces something similar to a work of art.

But where are the emotions, what aspect of this formula has engaged the poet's attention? The feelings, broadly, are delight and mistrust, evoked by an unsheathed, involuntary perception, and by a voluntary, questioning choice to "fence back" the abundance of such perception. The poem's energy is devoted to defining the relation, suspicious yet loving, between conscious intelligence and the mute, unconscious world from which it chooses its materials. That unconscious world is divided into the exterior world of things and the interior world of "habit," or unconscious, repeated action, which is a kind of reflection of the world of things within ourselves. "Habit" is like the world: unreflecting in the sense of "thoughtless," and full of reflections in the sense of varying repetitions. As such, "habit" mediates between mind and nature. It is like a part of nature within our-

selves, and insofar as it results from our accumulated choices—
or reflects them—it is like our mind that chooses and defines.
Language itself is a part of habit. The poem is not simply about
poetry, or about "aesthetics," but about memory and dreaming
as well.

If the poem, even more than certain poems by Stevens,
seems possibly "cold" or unsatisfying in some other way, then
the reason may lie less in the somewhat impersonal subject than
in the procedure. It is, perhaps, too discursive for some tastes.
I will try to explain what I mean, by contrasting the method of
"Reflections" with another poem on a similar subject, a poem
that I think deliberately avoids the discursive method. Here is
W. S. Merwin's "Whenever I Go There":

> Whenever I go there everything is changed
>
> The stamps on the bandages the titles
> Of the professors of water
>
> The portrait of Glare the reasons for
> The white mourning
>
> In new rocks new insects are sitting
> With the lights off
> And once more I remember that the beginning
>
> Is broken
>
> No wonder the addresses are torn
>
> To which I make my way eating the silence of animals
> Offering snow to the darkness
>
> Today belongs to few and tomorrow to no one

It is possible to think of the way this poem proceeds—elliptical, allusive, dark, introspective, abrupt, intimate—as a "contemporary" mode distinct from the more traditional method of "Reflections," with its "we," its transitions, similes, and repetitions, its distinct division between the images of bridge or ice on the one hand and the more discursive, explanatory passages. Moreover, Merwin's style seems designed, in part, to avoid some aspects of the other method. That is particularly true of the way Tomlinson's natural images are embedded separately in the abstract or linear exposition.

For that reason, some explicit exposition of the Merwin poem may be helpful. "There" seems to be an internal place, and a region of the mind that the poet chooses repeatedly to visit; knowledge of that place seems necessary to his imaginative life. But "habit" or expectation is useless in this place that never repeats itself. If "there" is the starting place for one's poems, or most valued perceptions, it is an absolute starting place: remembered categories and labels, if not quite discarded, must be subjected to new learning. If not quite futile, the stamps and titles and portraits and reasons must be subjected to a strange new sense of the particular wounds and fluidity and harsh light of the new, particular reality. To put it more simply, each time the poet meditates upon—say—the fact that in some cultures mourners wear white, his sense of the reasons must be new.

The life there is hidden in a nearly impenetrable darkness, and the effort even to describe it is awkward, somewhat farcical, cruelly exposed: the stamps, titles, professors, and portrait are the somewhat graceless manifestations of the conscious mind. The casualness or silliness of "sitting with the lights off" is part

of this comic treatment of the intelligence—a pedantic, inno-
cent entity, like Alice.

Having used the word "awkward" to describe the conscious
intelligence as it is portrayed here, I should like to return to
Tomlinson's poem long enough to point out the awkward or
uncomfortable air of its writing. Tomlinson survives, even ex-
ploits, the painful air of such tortuous discursive phrases as
"We, since no mirrors. . . ." The exposition, drawing its labori-
ous connections of idea and sequence, strains self-consciously
to deal with the particular, sufficient grace of the images them-
selves. The manner is perhaps just a little like a far different
kind of writing, the *mock*-discursive manner of Ashbery and
O'Hara.

Merwin, in contrast, is not uncomfortable; his elliptically
"beautiful" phrases fall with a stylistic ease that we do not ques-
tion even while we are questioning whether those phrases mean
anything. But, as he remembers "once more," his presence in
the realm of unreflecting perception is perpetually interrupted
and begun again. Each time one dreams, there is an arrival at a
new shore.

Dream, art, or meditation, the process he uses to get "there"
must be described as Romantic: it involves silence, and taking
on (or in) that aspect of unreflecting animals, and it is named
by reference not to thought, or even to action, but to the natu-
ral—and unreflecting—act of eating. In this dark, deep silence
the poet offers to the blankness of night the complementary
blankness of snow. If the night is total, if this desired realm is
as totally "blind" and "without habit" as seems to be true, then
the two blanknesses will be identical and continuous. This is
Keats's "already with thee": the unconsidering mind in the

unconsidering landscape, at one. It is like the blank of Arnold's sky and sea in "Self-Dependence," but without the boat—or, perhaps, the "Self."

So in a sense this poem embodies an extreme Romanticism: a pursuit of darkness, of silence, of the soul moving in ways so unlike abstract thought that it burrows into or "eats" its immobile paradise. On the other hand, the Romanticism is qualified by the form of the last line

Today belongs to few and tomorrow to no one

which, despite the absence of end punctuation, is a summarizing abstract formula. You could nearly call it a moral. In content, the formula is nominalistic: the present is difficult to perceive truly, without distorting it as most people do by seeing it in terms outside of it; the future is absolutely mysterious, and nothing of what we see now will help us in it. But Merwin must end his poem with a generality, and in fact the action of this poem, as with most of his best poems, is to create a generic experience. In this case, there is a generic archetype that covers "true memory" or "dreaming" or "making a poem" among other rough, too-explicit possibilities.

The difference between "Reflections" and "Whenever I Go There" is not one of "surrealism," then, or even of such hallmarks of "contemporary" diction as "snow" and "eating." Rather, the poems represent two ways of accommodating the Romantic and imagist traditions (which are part of the poet) to the nature of poetry, especially poetry's necessity to generalize. Tomlinson "fences back" the richness of nature and sleep with the habitual sentences and diction of modern poetry—and, perhaps, of literary criticism as well. He conveys the stresses of that process with an uncomfortable, nearly pedantic element of

discourse. Merwin attempts to create a generic reality abso-
lutely from particular poetic images and phrases, like an "echo
except that it is repeating no sound."[14] In effect, it is a generality
that has no other name but the poem—or, the abstract formula
that completes the poem.

In these paragraphs I have been using the expression "ge-
neric" to refer to a form in reality, distinct from generalizing in
language alone. In this light, poems like Merwin's "Come Back"
may be seen in terms other than "surrealism," which I under-
stand to refer to separate, self-enclosed realities like the reality
of a dream or the Freudian unconscious. Though it may also be
useful to think of such poems in terms of surrealistic images, I
think that the main idea of the poem is to establish an inclusive
form in life as a whole, while avoiding the appearance of ab-
stract definition:

Come Back

You came back to us in a dream and we were not here
In a light dress laughing you ran down the slope
To the door
And knocked for a long time thinking it strange

Oh come back we were watching all the time
With the delight choking us and the piled
Grief scrambling like guilt to leave us
At the sight of you
Looking well
And besides our questions our news
All of it paralyzed until you were gone

Is it the same way there

The emotions here apply whether "you" signifies a dead mother, or a lost person who was like a mother, or is as though dead; "there" is mostly death, but also an elsewhere that is like death. The terms are inclusive, generic. They are the terms of the poem partly because of the generic, dreamlike sort of experience about which the poet chose to write; but it is also true that they are the terms of the poem because they offer a way to write while fencing back the blind silence as little as possible.

IV. Conventions of Wonder

I. "Description": Bogan, O'Hara

It is time to look in more detail than I have so far, and in a different way, at the ongoing question of nature poetry—to use a loose, handy phrase. Emotionally, the question is how much credence we will give, and expect, when a poem expresses the feeling of wonder: respect or awe for natural creation. Poetically, the question is what tone or status we will find appropriate for the act of description. Description is the great rhetorical burden. In the riches and barrens of description the contemporary poem finds opportunities and temptations comparable to those of the seventeenth-century conceit, and limits more severely constricting than those of the heroic couplet. My assumptions about description will affect radically the world I see and the past I recall. As a poetic possibility, description is so pervasive that even to avoid it may demand an act of invention.

As first examples of these matters, here are two poems about grief; one of them is perhaps as traditional as possible in its method, while the other poem tries to stagger or confound an expectation at every turn. But the similarities are interesting: in relation to one tradition, the tradition of descriptive conventions, both poems find their poise by declining to be accepted at any point "as description." In their vastly different ways, both avoid the convention of words telling-about a physical reality; each poem implies the artificiality of such description; and each deflects our feelings about the physical world away from wonder, and toward impatience.

First, Louise Bogan's "Simple Autumnal":

> The measured blood beats out the year's delay.
> The tearless eyes and heart, forbidden grief,
> Watch the burned, restless, but abiding leaf,
> The brighter branches arming the bright day.
>
> The cone, the curving fruit should fall away,
> The vine stem crumble, ripe grain know its sheaf.
> Bonded to time, fires should have done, be brief,
> But, serfs to sleep, they glitter and they stay.
>
> Because not last nor first, grief in its prime
> Wakes in the day, and hears of life's intent.
> Sorrow would break the seal stamped over time
> And set the baskets where the bough is bent.
>
> Full season's come, yet filled trees keep the sky
> And never scent the ground where they must lie.

The gorgeously classic, even archaic details of the second quatrain do in their way allude to description, but we cannot see the generic fruit fall away, the generic vine stem crumble, the grain know its sheaf. (The figurative "know" is a further remove from description.) And the lines

> Sorrow would break the seal stamped over time
> And set the basket where the bough is bent

if they describe anything describe an engraving or allegorical frontispiece.

However, these are ancient ways of alluding to the physical world, and their conventions are older than modern poetry. In that ancient mode of writing about nature, one theme is a lament that the year will not delay; the technique is an emblematic, nearly allegorical use of natural images. But "Simple Autumnal" is something different from that: it is a modern poem, as well as a traditional sonnet about grief and time.

Thus, in its meaning the poem inverts the simple convention or commonplace: this grief does not complain that time, embodied by the seasonal and bodily cycles, gathers life in too soon. Sorrow rebels at having to endure a beginning, middle, and end in time. It is restless for a consummation; though life and time will be sequential, the poet's emotion seems to need them to be absolutely simultaneous, to be all over with at once. The sense of time is painful not simply because of mortality, but because of the "delay"—the process of successive stages.

In the familiar nineteenth-century relationship of poet and landscape, the poet's painful awareness of time is contrasted with a landscape that resists being a simple emblem, a nature whose features are aware neither of "delay" nor of "too-swift progress." Bogan's poem quietly brings that Romantic and modernist formula to bear upon the older formula of the autumnal lament. The older tradition is sharpened by a modernist sense of the speaker's isolated presence in the landscape, alien to it. The Romantic-modern tradition, contrasting the "mortal" intelligence with effectively "immortal" vegetation, is in turn tempered by the older formulary elements of the poem—and what those elements subdue is description. The slow sonnet movement and the stationary, firmly symbolic nature of the images, in other words, close off the cliché of the Romantic autumn landscape while using that landscape with a vividness that is not merely sonnet-like and symbolic. "Simple Autumnal" is not a great poem, but it is a poem of extraordinary, quiet poise.

Poise, and an impatience with the furnishings of the material world, also characterize Frank O'Hara's "Poem":

> The eager note on my door said "Call me,
> call when you get in!" so I quickly threw
> a few tangerines into my overnight bag,
> straightened my eyelids and shoulders, and
>
> headed straight for the door. It was autumn
> by the time I got around the corner, oh all
> unwilling to be either pertinent or bemused, but
> the leaves were brighter than grass on the sidewalk!
>
> Funny, I thought, that the lights are on this late
> and the hall door open; still up at this hour, a
> champion jai-alai player like himself? Oh fie!
> for shame! What a host, so zealous! And he was
>
> there in the hall, flat on a sheet of blood that
> ran down the stairs. I did appreciate it. There are few
> hosts who so thoroughly prepare to greet a guest
> only casually invited, and that several months ago.

The emotion is even less specified than Bogan's "grief" and "sorrow"—it is not merely unspecified, it is evasive, and the (evasive) relationship with the reader seems possibly more important than the emotional materials of the poem. There are the details that insist upon the unique, unpredictable character of experience ("tangerines," "jai-alai player") warning the reader that his generalities and expectations are likely to prove irrelevant to these irreducible particulars.

In fact, this is the kind of poem frequently described as "surrealist." Yet there is nothing in the details themselves—bright leaves, an overnight bag, the hall door—or in the action that violates the sense of reality; even the eyelids can be pictured naturalistically, with effort. The invitation appears, the response to it is interrupted by the coincidences and distractions of life for some months until, as the same coincidences and distractions have it, the belated visit coincides with disaster.

What O'Hara does systematically violate is a complacent sense of poetry. I mean not only the parodic "Oh fie!" and the equally parodic grammar (the deadpan construction of the last sentence, the drunkenly connective "but" of the seventh line); O'Hara also quarrels with our sense of how poetry treats experience. Most notably, this quarreling or teasing is embodied by the refusal to indicate whether the bloody corpse is figurative, or not. What matters, he implies, is the solipsistic poise at the poem's end. This poise and the strange road of transitions to it constitute, I suppose, what is "surrealistic" in the poem.

That surrealism, however, is not the subject or even the means, but rather the basis of the relationship between poet and reader. The reader is in effect cautioned that the poet's experience is as strange and perhaps unknowably special as the poem. Having accepted that cautionary distance, the reader can be assured that the gory disaster, the relationship, the human substance, however withheld, has not been forgotten or trivialized. To treat the experience as the poet has done, as a matter of personality, is not necessarily to neglect the experience, says the poet:

> I did appreciate it.

In one sense, the phrase means that each person takes his experience seriously in his own way.

Both the physical details and the "incident" of "Poem" could be described as mock-description. Before O'Hara can arrive at the crucial "I did appreciate it," with its implied italics on the second word, the reader must be led to wonder if the poet is a jackanapes who does *not* appreciate what he sees. Then O'Hara can contradict the reader who has doubted the poem's capacity for seriousness and wonder.

A mock-descriptive phrase like "the leaves were brighter than grass on the sidewalk" is not vague, or trite, or unconvincing so much as it is remote and bemused. It suggests an idiosyncratic experience of the natural world while also implying that which is probably idiosyncratic, and it suggests that writing that pretends to describe experience more directly and plainly is falsely conventional. As in Bogan's "Simple Autumnal," the vivid, insensate physical world serves to embody the painful stress between time as it is, objectively, and subjective human demands. Description that evokes wonder is a temptation because it asserts a marvelous harmony between the pace of the human mind and the pace of the world itself; but that harmony can be easy and untrue, forcing us to a synthetic pertinence or be-musement. The seal stamped over time is not so easily broken, or lived with, as the act of description would imply.

Certainly, both ways of tempering or avoiding description—Bogan's and O'Hara's—involve risks and limits. Bogan's poem relies on a frieze-like, contained pace and vocabulary, a formal poise some readers will find too serene for her materials. O'Hara, even in his best poems, courts the opposite difficulty of imitative form; these ephemeral, highly particular utterances all but collapse into the drugged listlessness of life, the sense of time's inertia that is what they often really are "describing," as in his "The Day Lady Died":

> It is 12:20 in New York a Friday
> three days after Bastille day, yes
> it is 1959 and I go get a shoeshine
> because I will get off the 4:19 in Easthampton
> at 7:15 and then go straight to dinner
> and I don't know the people who will feed me
>
> I walk up the muggy street beginning to sun
> and have a hamburger and a malted and buy
> an ugly NEW WORLD WRITING to see what the poets
> in Ghana are doing these days
>   I go on to the bank
> and Miss Stillwagon (first name Linda I once heard)
> doesn't even look up my balance for once in her life
> and in the GOLDEN GRIFFIN I get a little Verlaine
> for Patsy with drawings by Bonnard although I do
> think of Hesiod, trans. Richmond Lattimore or

Brendan Behan's new play or *Le Balcon* or *Les Nègres*
of Genet, but I don't, I stick with Verlaine
after practically going to sleep with quandariness

and for Mike I just stroll into the PARK LANE
Liquor Store and ask for a bottle of Strega and
then I go back where I came from to 6th Avenue
and the tobacconist in the Ziegfield Theatre and
casually ask for a carton of Gauloises and . . .

These addresses, malteds, and proper names are O'Hara's ver-
sion of "nature poetry." This chronicle, wavering ingeniously
between the pertinent and the bemused, tells of life's intent: the
weight of the day, sealed. It is what O'Hara meant by "abstrac-
tion" in language, as the word is used of painting—and the op-
posite of what the word has meant for poetry, the abstraction
of Wordsworth's "Ode to Duty." In that poem, description, with
its capacity for the arbitrary, the "sleep of quandariness," does
not govern the poet's way of speaking:

Through no disturbance of my soul,
Or strong compunction in me wrought,
I supplicate for thy control;
But in the quietness of thought:
Me this unchartered freedom tires;
I feel the weight of chance-desires:
My hopes no more must change their name,
I long for a repose that ever is the same.

This is the language of abstraction in the old sense. In a way, it
is even more alien to the universe we share with Bogan and
O'Hara than to the steadfast, abstract Duty it proposes.

It is necessary to quote the rest of "The Day Lady Died," in which O'Hara counters the sleepy, perspiring weight of "chance-desires" with a memory: a memory described, perhaps, but one that sets out to redeem the chance-desires of the day with something like "the quietness of thought." "To think," it is worth noting, is the verb introducing the memory:

> casually ask for a carton of Gauloises and a carton
> of Picayunes, and a NEW YORK POST with her face on it
>
> and I am sweating a lot by now and thinking of
> leaning on the john door in the 5 Spot
> while she whispered a song along the keyboard
> to Mal Waldron and everyone and I stopped breathing

Like Bogan's, this grief is bound to have a beginning, middle, and end; the means by which the poet tries to capture the emotion's "prime" as though it included the whole is a kind of description—an intense kind contrasted with the more numb, yet more explicit "description" that dominates most of "The Day Lady Died." My suspicion is that no poem in the collected works of Bogan or O'Hara—different as those two volumes are—escapes the act or possibility of description so totally as does the "Ode to Duty."

II. "Description": Some Contemporaries

Bogan's "Simple Autumnal" was written nearly fifty years ago, O'Hara's "Poem" approximately twenty-five. Do the issues I am trying to raise apply to more current work? The conventions of descriptive rhetoric persist, as I will try to show by looking briefly at examples from three books—each one the poet's second—published by relatively young poets in the last year or two.

The selection is arbitrary but, I hope, representative. The three volumes seem to me to present a range of sophistication about the practical, writerly problems of description; they embody a similar range of awareness as to the larger matters at stake. I will begin with the book that seems to me to demonstrate the least complex response to these matters, and conclude with the book that strikes me as most sophisticated—trying, on the way, to show that certain issues do indeed persist. The sources of my examples will be John Ratti's *Memorial Day,* David Steingass's *American Handbook,* and Charles Wright's *Hard Freight.*[1]

On a fundamental level, the shovel-and-pick matters of composition, the problem is the tyranny of adjective and simile; readers have seen them bent, well or poorly, to the poet's purpose many times. Even "good description" with "emotional force," after all this history, must be more than merely good in its rendering, and more than somewhat forceful in its feeling. Otherwise, the reader responds in an unsettled, grudging way, possibly with the half-formed uncharitable thought that the poem too weakly or innocently occupies a convention:

> Do you feel the speed of it?
> Do you hear
> the hum of this dreadful,
> beautiful hull hissing
> through the water?

The delicate bowsprit,
poised exquisitely,
is deadly
as a hawk's beak,
as knife-slit focused
as his eye . . .

The spider's web
of lines between us
cracks into place,
as taut as steel,
as dry as fire.
The royals, the topgallants,
the skysails
belly out,
and the fathoms
of black-green water
beneath us
are sliced open
by the endless speed
of the hull.

It is more than a little unfair to bring the weight of my concerns crashing heavily down upon these lines by John Ratti. (They are the opening and closing passages of his "Clipper Ship.") The writing is not awful, nor is the poem the best in his book *Memorial Day*. But, hoping that my attention will be taken as a measure of respect, I suggest that the modifiers ("dreadful," "exquisitely," "endless") and similes ("as taut as steel," "as a hawk's beak") fall short of their aim.

Moreover, this diction is not defective in itself. Rather, it "falls short" in the sense that it asserts a connection between a feeling—of cruel, irresistible beauty in patterns of physical action—and a physical reality—the hull and rigging moving through water and air; this assertion is too blatant, too familiarly worked. The familiarity and the blatancy, which make us apprehend and even accept the asserted connection, also make it fail to move us. It is the post-symbolist equivalent of Augustan personification, and not enough more than that.

I will try to support that harsh judgment with another example, one where pictorial art, and the visual picture's relation to "moral" matters in the widest sense of the word, play a considerable role. The painting-poem is a distinct contemporary genre, and one of the commonplaces of that genre consists of linking the idea of craft with the idea of reticence or indirection. Visual art is all description (in a sense), and its statement, compared to verbal statement, is implicit and indirect. A poem that in effect paraphrases a painting or a photograph is free both to use openly descriptive rhetoric and to use the large moral terms an ordinary description might preclude.

The idea of detachment, the artist's independence from his subject and even from his artifact, informs Ratti's poem "The Master's Eye: *Eakins' photograph of Bill Duckett*" where a concern that the poet might entertain is for the artist, in an ironic sense, "academic." The artist's craft is counterpoised as an almost puritanical force resisting or transforming eroticism:

> Whether or not
> excitement
> at being seen

has weighted
his penis
a bit
so that it falls
a little heavily
to the right
against his belly
is academic.
It is,
in fact,
the angle of his head
bowed in shadow,
the honest tension
in his right shoulder
and upper arm,
the slim
relaxed hand,
the perfect testicles
fallen against
his right leg
that explain
the fierce tenderness
in the master's
lidless eye.

That is, insofar as he is a "master," the artist's eye is the lens of a
camera; formal qualities alone interest the artist-as-master; the
erotic and personal aspects of experience are the concern of the
subject, and the speaker—and of the artist's audience with their
"academic" responses. That scheme is complicated by several

factors: the "lidless eye" of the lens implies another, more natural eye behind it; "master" suggests a sexual relationship within, or containing, the cool artistic relationship; the speaker seems to close off speculation about the erotic feeling in the picture, yet it is that feeling that seems to fascinate him—and so forth.

The objection is that the definitions and emphases become blunted or vague—evaded stylistically by the techniques and manners of description, philosophically by a merging of a formal ideal (*ut pictura poesis*) with the idea that emotional content is "impure," a matter for academic speculation. The language that is meant to be most faithful to the work of art—"the angle of his head," "shadow," "honest tension," "upper arm," "relaxed hand"—places us not in the photograph, but in an Art Appreciation lecture. The division between painter and poet, the formal and the sexual, is both simplistic and evasive, and the poem is, finally, a description of a description.

The poem's more ambitious, complex material depends too heavily upon the definition supplied by "lidless" and a few similar phrases. With only description and such terms—"fierce tenderness"—the emotional response hovers between a loose irony and a melodramatic knowingness. The abbreviated lines and "vivid" phrases flinch away from complexity, fall into the substitute of mere ambiguity. The potential subject is no less than the relationship between life and art, and one way to describe the problem is to observe that the poet has overestimated the possibilities of a conventional technique, the limits of an unmodified conventional genre.

Whatever limitations description may have, David Steingass's *American Handbook* demonstrates that a fresh, precise eye can do quite a lot. Take, for instance, his charming poem "Japanese TV" from the sequence called "Lotusbound"; some Sumo wrestlers are on television:

> Their feet
> Seem to rise from taproots,
> Their immense, stylized bodies
> Collide with medieval impact
> Among Peter's bansai pines
> And miniature porcelain.
> We sip warm sake. Suddenly their crouch
> Is Trout's, learning to walk!
> He breathes lightly as a finch in his crib.
> I try to plow the dark loam
> Between child and Sumo crouch,
> Before giving it to Peter, who will thrive there.
> But I am borne in a thimble of sake
> Snoring like a dog.

The thimble, the finch, the taproots all work: accurate and fresh. It is interesting that this appealingly dopey, lively poem escapes from the mechanical music of description partly by confronting explicitly some of the problems thereof: "I try to plow the dark loam. . . ." The dark, rich ground between two parts of a visual simile, the ground for explanation that will make the whole more than visual, and more than a simile, entails much. That fertile terrain entails not only the wrestlers and the infant, but the past, the poet's mind, and the mind of the auditor, who will thrive there.

"Japanese TV" plows beyond description just far enough to gesture in the direction beyond it, into the growth implied by

it. Outside of the sake-doze, and one's own mind, lies a medi-
tation on two images (wrestler and child)—perhaps on com-
bat, grace, posture, form. Partly, it is a poem about images, the
sluggishness and the activity that they can inspire. Though
the poem does not exactly set forth the ways of God to Man,
it is lucid and vivid—in its attitude as well as in its physical
details.

Many of the strengths and limitations of Steingass's genial,
open-faced, and conventional technique are epitomized for me
by his poem "The American Porch." The porch is the "Spreadea-
gle deck of an ark." Its wooden swing

                    poses generations
    Of black and white memory.
    The stiff lap sways like a metronome
    Through Sunday double-headers,
    Moves on any breeze
    As though someone has just left
    To shuck corn for supper,
    Or pitch sparks of dust between horseshoe stakes.
    Or set out for work
    On the sudden Monday morning
    Of the twentieth century

    Down the road that wound through bees
    In elderberries.
    Before the bend of those huge,
    Silent afternoons, you could look back
    Where percale curtains
    Hung listless as carp out the kitchen window.

Frizzled at the gills, a patriarch blue spruce
Shook hands over the rail, as everyone dozed
And thought he dreamed.
                                    You
Never return. Chances are
Malaria got you, or a war bride.
The anchor half of the century
Flowers to atomic proportions. Imagine—
A pygmy reduced your skull to essential size
And sewed your lips shut.

The stereotyped details of the first eight lines quoted—the swing, the corn-shucking, the horseshoes—are skillfully done, so skillfully that the reader, I think, feels inclined to accept the passage for all its sentimentality; those lines do work, as a kind of fond, open embrace of their own Capra-like clichés. And if it does succeed, then such fondness ought to be trusted, ought to be vigorous enough to imply its own "distance" or reservations. However, the poet strains after such distance by closing the poem's first section with the horribly banal lines:

Or set out to work
On the sudden Monday morning
Of the twentieth century

—a far worse kind of cliché, which spoils the mild virtues of the preceding nostalgic description without making the description any less sentimental. The first section of the poem thus closes with the silly false "perspective" of a cheap documentary film. As in certain films, a "voice over" tries to force the visual material beyond itself.

The point I am trying to make is only superficially similar to the traditional Imagist condemnation of "abstract commentary" or "moralizing." On the contrary: the problem is that the poem declines any explicit, abstract definition of its point of view. Instead, we are asked to take two separate kinds of cliché—the "sweet" and the "bitter"—ironically, and as a result the tone wobbles. Two figures of speech, or rather eight lines of description and a three-line figure of speech, are given too heavy a conceptual burden.

The kind of poetic turn or solution I am objecting to is neither unique nor accidental. In relation to "The American Porch," it is worth pointing out that the poem as a whole repeats the movement (as in the first section) from a relatively effective catalogue of descriptive commonplaces to a short closing passage of facile bitterness:

> you could look back
> Where percale curtains
> Hung listless as carp out the kitchen window.
> Frizzled at the gills, a patriarch blue spruce
> Shook hands over the rail, as everyone dozed
> And thought he dreamed.
> You
> Never return. Chances are
> Malaria got you, or a war bride.
> The anchor half of the century
> Flowers to atomic proportions. Imagine—
> A pygmy reduced your skull to essential size
> And sewed your lips shut.

It is not that the double meaning of "atomic" and the shrunken-head metaphor are bad in themselves; in themselves they are "good writing," not inferior to Steingass's pretty evocation of the kitchen window; but the last images of the poem are appended like an Aesopian moral to the happily indulgent description, with its multiplied details, its amiable toying with triteness. The tone of social criticism succeeds the tone of nostalgia mechanically, like an insincere apology. Though the poet's indignation at what has happened to the American porch is probably as heartfelt as his nostalgia for it, the descriptive method focuses the nostalgia as it cannot focus the indignation.

Finally, I would like to draw a series of examples from Charles Wright's book *Hard Freight*, dwelling on Wright's poems at somewhat greater length because I take his work to be particularly representative of much contemporary practice in the art, as practiced by gifted "younger" poets.

Hard Freight is the work, I think it fair to say, of a more sophisticated writer than Ratti or Steingass. I mean "sophisticated" in two senses: first, that his poems incorporate awareness of a wider range of possibilities, and second, that some of those possibilities draw upon the practice of other contemporary writers. Some of the stylistic attributes I have in mind will be dealt with later in this book; in relation to the present topic of description, Wright tests the application of that term to a complex and urbane poetic style.

That style, in *Hard Freight*, forms poems rich in impressive figures of speech and resourceful rhythms, and they are unified by a peculiar, consistent tone: bitter, controlled yet bardic. It is as though the constant, unrelaxing stream of dense poetic language is the only way to relieve the painful memories and bad forebodings that are Wright's characteristic materials.

The method is both exemplified and described by Wright's "Homage to Arthur Rimbaud"; Rimbaud's death and life and self all rise "invisible as fever," leaving behind

> Syllables, flowers, black ice;
> The exit, the split cocoon ...

Often the style of *Hard Freight* is so clotted with figures of speech ("Locked in their wide drawer, the pike lie still as knives"; "The door to the grass is closed"; "Its sky, old empty valise") that everything else is in danger of vanishing into the brocade. One form of this dense technique is the contemporary version of the catalogue, or formulaic litany:

> The heart is a hieroglyph;
> The fingers, like praying mantises, poise
> Over what they have once loved;
> The ear, cold cave, is an absence,
> Tapping its own thin wires;
> The eye turns in on itself.

If the parts here do not quite overwhelm the whole, they certainly risk doing so.

Wright appears to understand that risk perfectly well; moreover, he is willing to ignore it, as is suggested by the poem entitled "Synopsis" and placed at the end of the book's main section. In "Synopsis," the nexus between abstraction and image rests on the diagrammatical preposition "of," in the Smartian litany style of contemporary poetry:

> The white crow of belief
> The finger of speechlessness
> The eggshell of solitude
>
> The needle of lethargy
> The black glove of reprieve
> The toad of anticipation
>
> The spider of nothingness
> The damp stone of unknowing
> The wasp of forgetfulness

This poem is not on a risky borderline; rather, it crosses over into a kind of deliberate and solemn self-parody. That is, the technique is full circle from allegory: not because the abstract terms in the right half of each line denote mostly passive and negative states, but because the objects in the left half of each line bear all of the force, energy, concentration, and definition. That is, the linking "of" is full of irony, shadowed by the implication that the states of mind do not really have the vigor and integrity of outline that belong to the images. One can (or could) describe a toad, but not anticipation.

In other words, allegory often implies the confident attitude toward abstractions of a philosophical realist; "Synopsis" implies the pessimism in these matters of a philosophical nominalist. The dark mood and the dark method, packing each symmetrical rift with ore, are frankly and perversely reductive: a synopsis. The reader is invited by the poet to share in the grim joke of reduction, elegantly carried out.

A different, and I think better, strain in Wright's work appears when the writing is plainest, when it struggles with definition most directly, as in the third poem from his "Firstborn" sequence:

> You lie beside me now,
> Ineffable, elsewhere still.
> What should one say to a son?
>
> Emotions and points of view, the large
> Abstractions we like to think
> We live by—or would live by if things
>
> Were other than what they are;
> Or we were; or others were;
> If all were altered and more distinct?
>
> Or something immediate,
> Descriptive, the virtuous use of words?
> What can one say to a son?

Quiet—nearly to the point of vanishing—as these lines are, they do rather a lot, and do even more in the context of the entire sequence. The poet here understands that emotions and points of view are "abstractions" drawn from the particulate swirl of experience. At the same time, the "Descriptive" seems attractive and "virtuous." The point of the proliferating style, then, seemingly is to mediate between "the large/ Abstractions" and the "Descriptive," which is itself abstract and contrived in comparison to the "ineffable, elsewhere" circumstances of life.

Clearly, this poem is particularly appropriate grist for the mills I have been working. But it is not simply that the poem just quoted happens to use the word "descriptive" (and neither, I believe, does what I am saying apply uniquely to Charles Wright). Repeatedly, he finds his most compelling voice when the described locale and the foliating poetic language are balanced by their relation to some moral abstraction—often an abstraction simultaneously hollow and powerful, like "Salvation" in these lines about a childhood Bible camp:

> From 6 to 6, under the sick Christ,
> The children talk to the nothingness,
> Crossrack and wound; the dark room
> Burns like a coal, goes
> Ash to the touch, ash to the tongue's tip;
> Blood turns in the wheel:
> Something drops from the leaves; the drugged moon
> Twists and turns in its sheets; sweet breath
> In a dry corner, the black widow reknits her dream.
> Salvation again declines,
> And sleeps like a skull in the hard ground,
> Nothing for ears, nothing for eyes;
> It sleeps as it's always slept, without
> Shadow, waiting for nothing.
>
> ("NORTHANGER RIDGE")

The force of the idea—or rather of the hollow, ghost-idea—of salvation gives the descriptions their manic, twisting force. Without the obsessive Christian idea, the skull—as an image of mortality, say—would be merely melodramatic. As an unparaphrasable, stylishly surrealist image, the drugged moon that twists in its sheets is merely ornamental; but as an image of the confused, weird way these half-addled children experience the natural world from the center of this camp, the phrase tells us something. To put it simply, as a description of the moon, it is mannerism, but as the reflected force of a mental state, it is genuine.

Mannerism of a current kind often threatens Wright's poems. Yet even the somewhat slick gestures that go with the style of the moment reveal the concern with finding a means or partial substitute for abstract discourse—as in the capitalized mock-allegorical phrases that at times interrupt a description: in one poem, "the long, long waters of What's Left" and in another the figure of "Whatever Will Come/ His shoulders hunched under lost luggage." It is strange how such up-to-the-minute manner-isms express old needs like the need for allegory; or, consider this riddling catalogue of abstract nouns, "goods" that are kept in camphor:

> I walked these roads once, two steps
> Behind my own life, my pockets stuffed with receipts
> For goods I'd never asked for:
>
> Complacency, blind regret; belief;
> Compassion I recognized in the left palm;
> Respect, slick stick, in the right:
>
> One I have squandered, one
> I have sloughed like a cracked skin; the others,
> Small charms against an eventual present,
> I keep in the camphor box

("SKY VALLEY RIDER")

The passage, with its characteristic appositioned epithets ("respect, slick stick"), represents the need to generalize, the need to use abstractions, as dealt with by a quite contemporary version of nominalist rhetoric, a strangely oblique allegory: an allegory where the abstract terms seem to be merely in, rather than entirely of, their context. Like figures in a landscape, the abstract terms are figures in the pointedly alien terrain of description.

In such ways, Wright's best poems provide a fair example of a certain kind of poem written by able young contemporary poets. One aspect of his "Sky Valley Rider" and "Northanger Ridge" (and of "The American Porch," and for that matter of Ratti's "Clipper Ship," too) is that the locale tends toward the generic and the inward. The point of view is correspondingly unspecified, establishing a theater for the poem rather like that of many by Stevens—though without Stevens's bold use of abstract, even philosophical, diction. All of this allows the poet to use, as in "Northanger Ridge," a wide range of surreal or "deep" figurative language, a free bardic roaming for metaphor.

The opposite procedure is exemplified by Williams's "The High Bridge above the Tagus River at Toledo," in which the description restricts itself to a single, highly specified locale; the language is reportorial and objective; the point of view remains clearly that of a young man who does not speak the language, on the narrow bridge with the sheep, dogs, and shepherd—until the closing lines of the gradually deepening scene, when the point of view is further defined as revery and retrospect:

The whole flock, the shepherd and the dogs, were covered
   with dust as if they had been all day long on the road.
The pace of the sheep, slow in the mass,
governed the man and the dogs. They were approaching
   the city at nightfall, the long journey completed.

   In old age they walk in the old man's dreams and still walk
      in his dreams, peacefully continuing in his verse forever.

Now, the limitations of this gorgeous, involved simplicity are
clear; that is, one can see why Steingass or Wright or anyone
else might want to *include* more than Williams's magnificent
poem does. Nor can one presume to complain that a writer
pursues this direction or that one—a surrealist variety, or his
own personality—rather than some other scope or focus. Wil-
liams limited his description one way, another poet chooses
another.

   But just the same, the areas where Williams's poem sets out
to be reticent or loquacious are utterly clear; what is it that the
contemporary rhetoric leaves out? "Statement" is one term that
tempts me here. I have been using the flat, colorless word "de-
scription" partly in order to counterbalance another mild term:
discourse, discursiveness, the sound of the writer ambling or
running through his subject and speaking about it. As I will
explain in more detail further on, it is this declarative, prose
quality that seems cramped or excluded by the conventions at
hand. In a way, it is a matter of Williams's poem commanding
more of the freedoms of prose.

   To make a further, negative definition of what I mean, I will
quote Wright's "The New Poem," a merely fashionable poem in
Hard Freight:

The New Poem

It will not resemble the sea.
It will not have dirt on its thick hands.
It will not be part of the weather.

It will not reveal its name.
It will not have dreams you can count on.
It will not be photogenic.

It will not attend our sorrow.
It will not console our children.
It will not be able to help us.

This is the trite style and doctrine of nominalism unexamined and self-satisfied, the stuff of contemporary Contemporary Writing. In this month's *Poetry* magazine, Lawrence Raab writes of "The Word":

Is it the one we need?
Will it cure our dreams?

But we are afraid and tremble
before it.

Where does it come from—Nothing.
What will it deliver—Nothing.
What does it want—More.

More than you own.
More than you can possibly afford.[2]

Without flying too far off the handle, I suggest that in its oblique way this is cant.

The poem, new or old, should be able to help us, if only to help us by delivering the relief that something has been understood, or even seen, well. Restating such worthy, vital old slogans is my consolation and excuse for attempting, as I have done, to take up contemporary work and deal with it in the harsh perspective of history.

III. Wonder and Derangement: "Orchids," "Badger," and "Poppies in July"

"Wonder" is an inclusive name for our most significant feelings in response to nature, an abrupt and non-referential awe. It is an emotional term, as "description" is a rhetorical term. Wonder is non-referential in the sense that as a feeling it seems unrelated, by cause or analogy, to the rest of life. It seems pure. On the other hand, in attempting to tell about it, writers have needed to put wonder into analogous and causal relationship with other experiences. And in telling about other experiences—loss, love, mortality, praise of empire, despair, sexual eagerness—writers have used the experience of wonder, as an analogy and even as cause or result.

Using Keats's "Ode to a Nightingale," I have already tried to illustrate the persistence of these matters in modernist and contemporary poems, a persistence one can trace through an enormous, inventive variety of poetic styles. Before looking in the next chapter at some poems that largely ignore or evade the Romantic persistence, it remains necessary to sketch in some broad historical distinctions. That is, returning for a moment to another nineteenth-century example, I would like to ask how some of the conventions of wonder have changed. The changes are in the expectations of readers as well as in the poetry.

My examples will surround a somewhat peculiar theme: namely, the way wonder interacts with a deranged or neurasthenic aspect of personality. As in the ordinary phrase, wonder takes the distressed personality "out of himself." Or, does it take the distress out, putting it into the object of wonder? Such questions may be dealt with by the sensible, conservative idea of "objectivity." In the present context, that idea involves the use of objective natural reality to clarify a difficult state of mind. A "sane" work of art in this sense accomplishes its meaning consciously. Otherwise the meaning is the reader's creation, the art a symptom; sanity in writing would be the tonal adjustment that changes confession into character-making. Authentic clarity is the style's proof that the fiction is true: not a patient's tortured, oblique version of a dream, but the authoritative dream itself, naked and magisterial.

These values are tested, and perhaps vindicated, by the most striking poems by the nineteenth-century mad poet (and peasant-poet) John Clare. In these poems the emotional resonances of natural images are used to manage dark, aberrant materials. In most of them, the basic fiction is small and violent: various forms of animal life struggle for a precarious, often treacherous, shelter. Clare seems to show with all but cold precision what was otherwise too painful for him to face.

The result is a strange mood of obsession and objectivity, a mood compelling enough to rise above the defects of "Badger," probably the best-known poem of the group:

> When midnight comes a host of dogs and men
> Go out and track the badger to his den,
> And put a sack within the hole, and lie
> Till the old grunting badger passes by.

He comes and hears—they let the strongest loose.   5
The old fox hears the noise and drops the goose.
The poacher shoots and hurries from the cry,
And the old hare half wounded buzzes by.
They get a forked stick to bear him down
And clap the dogs and take him to the town,   10
And bait him all the day with many dogs,
And laugh and shout and fright the scampering hogs.
He runs along and bites at all he meets:
They shout and hollo down the noisy streets.

He turns about to face the loud uproar   15
And drives the rebels to their very door.
The frequent stone is hurled where'er they go;
When badgers fight, then every one's a foe.
The dogs are clapt and urged to join the fray;
The badger turns and drives them all away.   20
Though scarcely half as big, demure and small,
He fights with dogs for hours and beats them all.
The heavy mastiff, savage in the fray,
Lies down and licks his feet and turns away.
The bulldog knows his match and waxes cold,   25
The badger grins and never leaves his hold.
He drives the crowd and follows at their heels
And bites them through—the drunkard swears
      and reels.

The frightened women take the boys away,
The blackguard laughs and hurries on the fray.   30
He tries to reach the woods, an awkward race,
But sticks and cudgels quickly stop the chase.

He turns agen and drives the noisy crowd
And beats the many dogs in noises loud.
He drives away and beats them every one,   35
And then they loose them all and set them on.
He falls as dead and kicked by boys and men,
Then starts and grins and drives the crowd agen;
Till kicked and torn and beaten out he lies
And leaves his hold and cackles, groans, and dies.[3]   40

Because some readers of contemporary poetry may find Clare's poem dull and cramped stylistically, I will say something about "Badger" itself, before trying to show how comparison with Clare can illuminate the way we read a poet like Roethke.

"Badger" has certain characteristic, fairly obvious faults. It appears to buy an effect of painful reticence by sacrificing fluidity. The rather unvarying sentence structure, cramped rhythms, repetitious rhymes, and confined diction might be blamed on the bad education of a peasant-poet. On the other hand, with more formal schooling Clare might have been content with still more of the Augustan literary formula that mars lines seventeen and twenty-five. In a similar way, plain stylistic elements like the "noise" root and the word "beats" might seem crude or wooden in these lines:

He turns again and drives the noisy crowd
And beats the many dogs in noises loud.
He drives away and beats them every one,
And then they loose them all and set them on.

But these repetitions, flat from one point of view, are the technical driving principle of the poem—a powerful, supple resource, in fact, for it contributes simultaneously to two difficult, opposed tones: an air of stubbornly strict, flatly unrhetorical truth, and an air of rage. The "roughness" of repetition and monotonous line is genuinely unsentimental, yet emotionally wider than mere reportage.

The source of the pent energy or rage is illustrated by the lines just quoted, which repeat the word "beats" in successive lines. Earlier, in line twenty-two, the badger "beats them all," and at the end he

> starts and grins and drives the crowd agen;
> Till kicked and torn and beaten out he lies
> And leaves his hold and cackles, groans, and dies.

The earlier "bites" and "bait," because they are monosyllabic verbs of nearly the same sound, also contribute to the effect of this repetition; he beats them, repeatedly, but loses.

The verb "drive" is repeated five times in the last two stanzas. And if one wants to see how Clare prolongs and builds his reticent description so powerfully, the best way may be to trace the verbs, especially the monosyllabic verbs. Apart from participial forms like "grunting," the first six lines contain eleven active verbs. This high incidence of inflected verbs, resulting in a slow, distinctly accented line, also results in a crackling sense of action—so that the peculiar method of the poem develops its peculiar double tone. Several brief passages sustain an *average* of three verb forms to a line, as with "starts and grins and drives" above. "Grins," like "drives" and "beats," is repeated: those three words, and the way their repetitions are managed, convey the force of the poem's feeling and embody its structure. In plot as well as in sentence, though the style seems stationary the scene breathes and moves with a disturbing, eager violence of energy.

Aside from attractions and limitations of technique, the poem presents less apparent problems of aspiration and conception. Its special approach to the relation between natural detail and emotion is particularly relevant to the present general subject. John Keats, through a letter to Clare from their common friend and publisher John Taylor, provides a suggestive formulation:

> If he recovers his strength he will write to you. I think he wishes to say to you that your Images from Nature are too much introduced without being called for by a particular Sentiment—To meddle with this subject is bad policy when I am in haste, but perhaps you conceive what he means.[4]

If Taylor's paraphrase is at all accurate, then Keats in this instance is on the side of explicit statement, or at least of paraphrasable, reasonably explicit "Sentiment."

A host of distortions and confusions recur around the relative status in poems of "Images from Nature" on the one hand and "Sentiments" on the other. Clare's remark that he "found the poems in the fields" must be taken figuratively as a way of saying that he found their materials in the fields; that might seem hardly worth saying if it were not for such naive versions of imagism as the following, inspired by Clare's statement and the false implication that poems exist outside of the mind, "in the fields":

> An object or incident in life arouses an overwhelming emotion in him, and a desire to express the emotion. The

> crystallization is, as it were, automatically accomplished;
> for the only way he can communicate his emotion is by
> describing the objects that aroused it. If his emotion was
> a true one, the vividness and particularity of his descrip-
> tion will carry it over to us. . . . Thus, quite simply, the
> cause of the emotion becomes the symbol. The miracle is
> accomplished.[5]

"Description" here seems to be conceived, simplistically, as
mere transmission of experience—as though Clare did nothing
but witness the badger-baiting and then *convey* it. Crude though
the fallacy may be, it presents a recurring question for poetry. I
dwell upon a mistaken version of Clare's procedure in order to
emphasize that he is the sort of poet likely to suggest such an
explanation. That is, his use of physical detail is far more sug-
gestive, conceptually, than explicit—as in many modern poems.
However, he is not a modern poet, just as he is not a mere su-
perseded primitive.

The remarks just quoted have their opposite or complemen-
tary position, a position somewhat like the one suggested by
Keats on "Images from Nature." That is, by our various inge-
nious means, we might be able to explain away or pardon the
pathetic fallacy, but the objection of a literalist retains its force:
we have an intensely written poem, nearly twice as long as Jon-
son's "To Heaven," about very little. Tone, one aspect of which
is length, is so much in excess of the apparent stimulus in "Bad-
ger" that the poem must be defended, if not from the charge of
insanity, then from that of sentimentality.

Neither charge, I think, occurs except theoretically; when
actually reading the poem, we experience the peculiarly disci-
plined tone of intense suffering, and—especially on successive

readings—an air of authenticity, an intuitive sense of no fallacy between the description and the emotion.

And yet, by questioning the grounds whereby "Badger" links its images from nature with its emotions, we can discover a surprising artfulness of execution, and a conception that is solid in ways worth studying. To show what I mean, here is a contemporary poem, Theodore Roethke's "Orchids"; it can be seen as a poem late in the modernist tradition whose roots are in the questions of "Sentiments," "Images from Nature," and poems "found in the fields." For many contemporary readers, "Orchids" may seem a more plausible poem than "Badger," more clearly a good poem—especially on the first reading or two. But whether my suspicion that "Orchids" has more of the look of a good poem, for a contemporary reader, is true or false, the comparison is instructive—for matters of persuasiveness of effect and shrewdness of procedure:

Orchids

They lean over the path,
Adder-mouthed,
Swaying close to the face,
Coming out, soft and deceptive,
Limp and damp, delicate as a young bird's tongue;
Their fluttery fledgling lips
Move slowly,
Drawing in the warm air.

And at night,
The faint moon falling through whitewashed glass,
The heat going down

So their musky smell comes even stronger,
Drifting down from their mossy cradles:
So many devouring infants!
Soft luminescent fingers,
Lips neither dead nor alive,
Loose ghostly mouths
Breathing.

Roethke's free verse is end-stopped and slow, and like Clare's poem this one moves in rather small grammatical units; but the predominance of active verbs that characterizes "Badger" is reversed in "Orchids." The last five lines are largely a list of substantives, for example, and lines two through four are a list of modifiers.

This suspended, almost unpredicated syntax could be referred to static or passive attributes of the object; but it works primarily to help voice the speaker's feeling. He is obsessed, nearly overwhelmed, and more caught up by the object and its qualities than by statements he could predicate about them.

And the same emotional direction is suggested by the poem's other notable stylistic parts. The present tense, for example, works oddly with the two-part, day-then-night structure; the effect is to suggest reverie, which is a mental process, yet to maintain the natural object's dominance over the mental process. Similarly, the rhythm moves in slow, short, equal spasms, heavily defined by pronounced pauses and consonances ("soft and deceptive,/ limp and damp"), a movement that suggests absorbed helplessness. A sort of enervated panic aroused by the unconscious life of the natural object becomes, by the poem's last word, so insistently suggested that we might call it explicit. The emotion of defeated hysteria emerges as an emphatic surrender of the poet's voice to the physical scene.

"Badger" and "Orchids" have in common the general technique of description, and also an experience: wonder, the experience of fascination with a physical scene—its cruelty and its persistent unconsciousness. (Of course, that is the perhaps obvious answer for the literalist: the experience in "Badger" is not the baiting, but the poet's experience of figuratively being the badger.) The badger is the one who deserves to win, but loses, the being who "beats" until he is "beaten out." The wonder is at the "grinning," unreflecting energy of the scene, with its pattern of unjust defeat. The poet both engages and implicitly examines his fierce, perhaps helpless, identification with nature.

Both poems, then, render the experience of being dominated by a metaphor—and by the unsuitable, unlike parts of it: orchids are like human life, but, not conscious, they have an eerie persistence that is both repellently and hypnotically nonhuman. And the badger's agony is like human suffering; here, however, the distinction from human life is explicit and pervasive, while the affinity with human life builds invisibly and by implication. It builds through the workmanlike exposition as if it were a ringing in the ears.

I have pointed out how Roethke's poem elaborates the emotions he wants to associate with the orchids, underlining the emotion with its syntax, its rhythm, the arrangement of its parts. Clare's method is more indirect, more tactful and cumulative—a fact most apparent in the matter of diction. The striking choices of word in "Orchids" tend to be affective and anthropomorphic: "deceptive," "delicate," "devouring," "ghostly." In "Badger," too, the most notable moments in the diction suggest human life, but more quietly and subtly. One explanation of the subtlety is that the anthropomorphic words also have a purely descriptive aspect, a descriptive aptness approximated only by the rather pedestrian "delicate" of the four modifiers from "Orchids" quoted above. In "Badger," the word or phrase with human or emotional overtones also subdues those overtones by its purely descriptive justice: "grunting" (line 4), "demure" (line 21), "grins" (line 26), "awkward" (line 31), "starts" (line 38), "cackles" (line 40). In short, Roethke embraces the pathetic fallacy easily and openly, while Clare avoids it, or at least quietly skirts it.

To summarize, the poem "Orchids" takes the fusion of emotion with the natural object as an accepted starting point: as granted. There is no gesture toward defining a literal, personal motivation for the emotion; neither does the poet try to suggest that the emotion is irresistibly part of the orchids—this is a frankly special sensibility or mood, and the poem consists of rhetorical elaboration of the emotion by means of description. Questions of motivation are meant to be disposed of by the convention or starting point of the poem.

The poem "Badger," in contrast, takes the fusion of emotion with the natural object as an eventual goal. And though the poet does not offer literal, personal motivations, his poem is a sustained effort to establish a powerful sense of irresistible, necessary connection between scene and feeling—exactly that sense of connection that Roethke's poem in effect asks us to accept without question. The elaboration of the orchids is explicit and rhetorical, and they exemplify, figuratively, a mood and a sense of life; but the agony of the badger is presented as an actual and self-sufficiently awful fate.

What does this difference in rhetorical procedure mean for the way each poem relates Romantic wonder to the sense of derangement or distress? "Orchids" emphasizes the powerful aspect of natural life that is quite alien to consciousness. The implied spectator of the badger-baiting is aware of this aspect of the physical world; it is what compels his reticent attention. But while "Orchids" insists upon the object's predominance in a manner (or convention) that emphasizes its own voice—obsessed and neurasthenic—Clare actually does keep the object predominant. And the voice could hardly be called neurasthenic; the tight, minimally varied pentameter proves surprisingly well-suited to the energetic, rapt observation of a natural scene—as is the case, in fact, in some of Roethke's early, descriptive poems. In one of these, "Heron," the bird

> stands in water where the swamp
> Has deepened to the blackness of a pool,
> Or balances with one leg on a hump
> Of marsh grass heaped above a musk-rat hole.
>
> He walks the shallow with an antic grace.
> The great feet break the ridges of the sand,
> The long eye notes the minnow's hiding place.
> His beak is quicker than a human hand.
>
> He jerks a frog across his bony lip,
> Then points his heavy bill above the wood.
> The wide wings flap but once to lift him up.
> A single ripple starts from where he stood.

The stiff texture that creates fluid life recalls Clare, particularly in the many poems about nesting, threatened animals written during the same period as "Badger":

> The hedgehog hides beneath the rotten hedge
> And makes a great round nest of grass and sedge,
> Or in a bush or in a hollow tree;
> And many often stop and say they see
> Him roll and fill his prickles full of crabs
> And creep away; and where the magpie dabs
> His wing at muddy dike, in aged root
> He makes a nest and fills it full of fruit,
> On the hedge bottom hunts for crabs and sloes
> And whistles like a cricket as he goes.
> It rolls up like a ball or shapeless hog
> When gipsies hunt it with their noisy dog;
> I've seen it in their camps—they call it sweet,
> Though black and bitter and unsavoury meat.

This is not identification, but wonder; and wonder is in its peculiar way a more matter-of-fact emotion, as the last line exemplifies.

It is, in a way, startling that wonder finds such complete and pure expression in end-stopped, slow pentameter lines, with symmetrical caesura and short, simple sentences. In Roethke's "Heron," wonder is simply directed at the point where the material world becomes animate. Clare uses the same stolid manner to suggest moral as well as visual fascination; it is as though Roethke combined the disturbed sensibility of "Orchids" with the pure, taciturn absorption of "Heron." The modern poet seems to need or prefer separate styles for emphasizing the moral and the visual aspects of wonder. In that separation lie the reasons why "Badger" seems larger and more profound than "Orchids."

To clarify that judgment, and to examine the apparent connection between wonder and derangement, I will make the Clare-Roethke comparison into a triangular one by adding Sylvia Plath's "Poppies in July." I think that the way each poet uses the pathetic fallacy and the feeling of wonder, as ways of writing about derangement, is instructive.

Poppies in July

Little poppies, little hell flames,
Do you do no harm?

You flicker. I cannot touch you.
I put my hands among the flames. Nothing burns.

And it exhausts me to watch you
Flickering like that, wrinkly and clear red, like the
    skin of a mouth.

A mouth just bloodied.
Little bloody skirts!

There are fumes that I cannot touch.
Where are your opiates, your nauseous capsules?

If I could bleed, or sleep!—
If my mouth could marry a hurt like that!

Or your liquors seep to me, in this glass capsule,
Dulling and stilling.

But colourless. Colourless.

If we compare the poppies as they are treated here with the orchids in Roethke's poem, it becomes clear that the assumptions about "Images from Nature" are quite different; "called for by a particular Sentiment," the hell flames are clearly, perhaps even insistently, figures of speech. Whereas Roethke's speaker seems overcome by the emotive qualities in the orchids, giving them anthropomorphic adjectives as if helplessly—"deceptive," "devouring," "ghostly"—Plath almost laboriously distinguishes the imaginary flames from the actual poppies:

> I put my hands among the flames. Nothing burns.

It almost looks like the amateurish rhetoric of a beginner, explaining the metaphors by drawing a picture for the reader. And yet this obsessive separating of the pathetic fallacy works; we see the poppies vividly, and feel the disturbance.

This difference between "Orchids" and "Poppies in July" can be described in both stylistic and moral terms. Stylistically, Plath's language is conservative and traditional; it nearly always is, perhaps because her poems need an accessible, familiar medium in order for the reader to feel the impact of other aspects of Plath's art. The language cannot be experimental, we are tempted to say, because the experience and the emotions are.

In any case, she says nothing that is not either literally true— "you flicker"—or a clearly and consciously subjective figure of speech—"little hell flames." That poppies furnish opiates is something one must know, not see. For all of its restlessness or hysteria, the poem's manner is information, the clarity of simile:

> wrinkly and clear red, like the skin of a mouth.

Roethke's "adder-mouthed" and "lips neither dead nor alive" convey the far different idea, as we have seen, that language has been taken over by the flowers themselves. Only his lines about "the heat going down" impart information without insisting on the pathetic fallacy. His poem is more dramatic. The derangement and the stylistic matter of the pathetic fallacy are merged.

And yet the sense of wonder, of awe at the mouthlike flowers' separate existence, pervades "Poppies in July." The ideas of violence, pain, and drugged sleep that the poppies embody are the "Sentiment" that "calls for" or justifies the image of poppies—at first. But as the poem progresses, it is the unconscious, neutral repose of the poppies that comes to dominate. They are red, but do not burn; flicker, but do not tire; contain opium, but do not even sleep. The ideas of death, hurt, or sleep are not so large or so blank as the bland infinite sleep of nature and its parts: "Colourless." The rhetorical and emotional "colours" that Roethke assigns to the flowers wholeheartedly, and that Plath teases and plucks nervously, amount to so much talk—compared to the wonder that in its final purest state belongs not to poetry but to silence. The poet's mouth cannot marry a "hurt" like the poppy's because the poppy is not a hurt, except in the mind.

In that sense, I think that Plath's poem illuminates and applies wonder in the same sense that Clare means when he uses the word repeatedly in "The Squirrel's Nest":

> . . . wondered strangely what the nest could be
> And thought besure it was some foreign bird,
> So up I scrambled in the highest glee,
> And my heart jumped at every thing that stirred.
> 'Twas oval shaped; strange wonder filled my breast;

> I hoped to catch the old one on her nest
> When something bolted out—I turned to see—
> And a brown squirrel pattered up the tree.
> 'Twas lined with moss and leaves, compact and strong;
> I sluthered down and wondering went along.

In its full dimension, the feeling of wonder persists beyond explanations, and absolutely beyond the marrying or "colouring" of other emotions. In the midst of the flowers or the badger as an emblem of pain, the object of wonder persists as an emblem of nothing at all.

That cold separateness explains the role of Romantic wonder in poems that deal with intolerable or deranged feelings. No matter how painful or disturbing the individual fate may be, the natural world supplies a balancing force just as inexorable. Thus, in the implicit background of "Badger," a fate prevails that might be called the unjust failure of an uncommon man. "He beats"— and "beats" repeatedly, drives all before him with astonishing energy, and loses anyway. The poet presents this grinning ferocity in defeat as frightful, at least as terrible as the eventual defeat. Thus, wonder at the badger's unthinking energy—*because* it is separate and alien, because the pathetic fallacy is justified, not assumed—becomes a way of defining, while expressing, extremes of pain.

What the physical evocation of the wrinkled poppy or grunting badger does, which abstract exposition could not do, is to reproduce something of the color and aura of contingency. The experience—being trapped in defeat, or in the glass capsule of isolation—includes the victim's bewildered sense of a swarm of events distracting but not deflecting his fate: as though even in the assurance of grim defeat there was a tormenting sense of accident, a coincidental doom. The evidence and metaphor for treacherous, multiple possibility as an element of experience is the world of things. Unconscious life is, as Roethke says, "devouring." Certain varieties of moral pain can be best evoked by a sense of the physical universe; and the emotional response to that distracting swarm is derangement, a violent sliding away of the belief that things cohere.

The quality I admire in "Badger" and "Poppies in July" is a kind of patience, an almost stolid taking up of obligations: primarily, to show how the "Sentiment" is linked to the "Images from Nature" and not merely to elaborate the "Sentiment"— however effectively. The link, the emotional vision of the object, is consciously defined and justified. I am aware that in valuing such definition more than the procedure of "Orchids," in which the link is taken for granted, I am preferring one convention to another.

There is a special quality of the poetic voice in the sturdy, persistent convention of "Badger" and of Plath's patient explanation: "I put my hands among the flames. Nothing burns." The quality is echoed—perhaps consciously—in Roethke's "Heron." As a way of dealing with the natural world, of telling about it, those earnest sentences represent one possibility within the wide range of discursiveness. I mean that Clare applies to the job of description something like the uncluttered, purposeful qualities of speech. I would now like to turn to the wider possibilities of that mode: the poet talking, predicating, moving directly through a subject as systematically and unaffectedly as he would walk from one place to another.

V. The Discursive Aspect of Poetry

I. "Earnestness": Cunningham, Bidart

Definitions of the term "discursive" tend to divide into two apparently contradictory senses. On the one hand, the word describes speech or writing that is wandering and disorganized; on the other, it can also mean "explanatory"—pointed, organized around a setting forth of material.

These opposites are reconciled by the radical sense of motion over terrain; the word signifies going through or going over one's subject. Whether digressively or directly, at a walk or at a run, the motion is on the ground and by foot, putting its weight part by part onto the terrain to be covered. Such a method tends to be inclusive; it tends to be the opposite of intuitive.

It even tends to be earnest; and another way to describe the quality in poetry that I mean by "discursive" is to say that it is primarily neither ironic nor ecstatic. It is speech, organized by its meaning, avoiding the distances and complications of irony on one side and the ecstatic fusion of speaker, meaning, and subject on the other. The idea is to have all of the virtues of prose, in addition to those qualities and degrees of precision that can be called poetic.

I don't think that this definition points toward a single kind of writing; rather, it suggests a quality that might appear in a surprisingly wide range of styles. I suspect that a wish to discourse fully about a variety of subjects—and not mere length, not a wish to be "large"—was one motive behind such various undertakings as Robert Lowell's three long books made up of unrhymed sonnets, Richard Howard's dramatic-historical poems, and John Berryman's *The Dream Songs*. Not epic bulk, but inclusiveness, a wish to include many of the mind's steps and many of its interesting travels, is an ambition these works share.

I have said earlier that much of the work by the so-called "New York poets" could be described as mock-discursive, a fact that further suggests the wide range of styles within which the quality I have in mind appears. Moreover, much of the most memorable writing by these poets seems to emerge when there is the least element of "mock" statement, the largest element of open discourse. Frank O'Hara's "In Memory of My Feelings," for example, despite its surrealist texture, is an extended essay on two related, rather abstract themes: the multiple nature of personality ("My quietness has a number of naked selves"), and the multiple past stirring within us ("The dead hunting/ and the alive, ahunted"). And though the feeling of O'Hara's poem is nominalistic, its method is leisurely and spacious, avoiding irony and ecstasy in the interest of a quality or goal related to statement: the quality poetry shares with prose and speech.

Berryman defines the goal this way:

> I'm through with Henry, but the minute I say that, pains
> course through me. I can't bear to be rid of that admirable
> outlet, that marvelous way of making your mind known
> to many other people.[1]

That is, Henry and the special manner of *The Dream Songs* are
"marvelous" and useful to the poet because of what they let him
say, and not as complex dramatic screens or personae. Reading
the quotation closely, we find that the poet treasures the ac-
complishment of "making your mind known": not the subject
alone, and not simply the subject plus the feelings that find their
"outlet," but both of those along with the mind itself, its way of
moving as well as the various grounds that support it on its way.

In relation to "other people," the goal thus emphasized is to
tell them what the mind thinks and feels, but also to have them
"know" the mind itself: where it finds itself, but also how it has
come there, its course. Such discourse does not absolutely ex-
clude irony or ecstasy; rather, it subordinates them to the idea
of "making your mind known." Both wittiness and revelation,
in such writing, may be sacrificed in the interest of that more
literal, plainer, and perhaps larger ambition.

In illustration, I will cite two poems that in most ways could not
be more unlike, either in technical matters like prosody or in
the quasi-political terms by which practice in the art is spuri-
ously divided into a conservative, academic "right" and a wilder,
experimental "left." To make a more solid distinction, one of the
poems has the inclusiveness of epigrammatic summary; the
other is inclusive by being relatively extended and like speech.

What the poems share is the tone and substance of earnestness, the pursuit of definition beyond the temptations merely to divert the reader or impress him. The pleasure in both cases is that of knowing someone's mind in the most precise and animated way: the soul, in other words, revealed in language.

The first poem is J. V. Cunningham's first epigram in the *Doctor Drink* series. In structure, the poem is compressed and reductive rather than spacious and exhaustive in the ways that might normally be associated with discursiveness; but what distinguishes Cunningham's epigram is an earnest, literal quality that is essential to what I hear as the element of discourse in poetry. Primarily abstract in diction, and composed in four couplets of tight iambic tetrameter, "Epigram #1" is also one contemporary poem that has nothing to do with nominalism, natural images and "the thing itself":

> In the thirtieth year of life
> I took my heart to be my wife,
>
> And as I turn in bed by night
> I have my heart for my delight.
>
> No other heart may mine estrange
> For my heart changes as I change,
>
> And it is bound, and I am free,
> And with my death it dies with me.

This uncompromising terseness can serve as a far-point or extreme example for one kind of discursive style. On the other hand, the clipped, deliberate movement is hardly unrhetorical; the poem might even seem melodramatic, if the definitions were not so concise and accurate. Nor does Cunningham set out to avoid irony altogether; the "delight" of the second couplet and the freedom of the last couplet are both severely qualified. The special accomplishment lies in the way that this qualifying irony acts as a hairline indicator for meaning, rather than an outlet into ambivalence or the elusiveness of "wit." The sexual and emotional solitude of line three is not simply lightened into sheer delight by the fact that the poet has his own emotions for colloquy and study. Yet just the same, there is a measure of delight in that commitment to introspection—or if not delight, then the dry rewards enumerated by the third and fourth couplets.

Unlike an actual wife, one's heart is beyond estrangement, divergence, and mortality. The line "And with my death it dies with me" recalls another "Epigramme," Ben Jonson's great poem "On My First Sonne":

> O, could I loose all father now. For why
> Will man lament the state he should envie?
> To have so soon scap'd worlds, and fleshes rage,
> And, if no other miserie, yet age?

The man who takes no actual wife escapes, if no other misery, yet bereavement or bereaving. These central lines of Jonson's poem meditate the conflict between possession and freedom, attachment and reason, life and peace, love and delight; and Cunningham, too, considers how "looseing" a profound human attachment can solve these conflicts. Jonson's poem is greater, partly because he brings both halves of the dilemma to a more intense pitch: he can neither cease feeling grief as a father, nor cease feeling the imperative to Christian resignation, neither be perfectly reasonable nor lose himself utterly beyond reason in a sense of loss. He cannot claim to have balanced the loss of his heart's best liking with the solace of Christian love for the child's immortal soul; but, compounded of both reason and emotion, he can vow to try to balance that liking and that love:

> all his vowes be such,
> As what he loves may never like too much.

The resolution takes its difficult ground equally distant from a smug consolation and an indulgent totality of grief.

It is a measure of how remarkable Cunningham's poem is, that it does not dwindle into complacency or triviality in the glare of such a comparison. The reason is that "Epigram #1," like Jonson's poem, earnestly shows us precisely what is in the poet's mind about paternity, or marriage, and their denial. The aspects of marriage enumerated by "Epigram #1"—estrangement, change, bereavement, bed—make up a remarkably thoughtful summary; they attain the goal of actually telling something about marriage; rather than a turn of wit or an impressively deep metaphor, we are offered something more like the effort at truth of an earnest conversation, an essay, or a letter on the same topic. Those kinds of discourse may be unlike the poem in style, and certainly are unlike it in structure, but they share the literalness of its conception and method. One way for me to put it is that Cunningham is "really" comparing marriage with an introspective solitude in the same way that Jonson is really making his mind known to us on the subject of a child's death. One need not reject all poems that are dramatic and figurative in conception in order to admire these for being personal and literal.

The plainspokenness of Cunningham, then, depends more upon the approach to the material and the reader than upon the structure of the poem. Moreover, in diction the poem is idiomatic rather than colloquial, and in rhythm it is uncompromisingly metrical. But discourse need not ramble, or converse; the terrain to be covered may be such that the statement will be summary and reductive. And in this case Cunningham's subject is the reduction of an expectation, marriage, to solitude, just as Jonson's subject is the reduction of "too much hope" to a vow in the direction of limit. In both poems, the statement naturally reaches toward the apex of summary.

The word "statement" makes the point plainly: these poems present abstract propositions rather directly, and the reader is likely to feel an urge to agree or disagree with such poems, as he agrees or disagrees with other statements. Cunningham presents a further degree of abstraction in his statement than Jonson does, for the event in "Epigram #1" is abstracted from the biographical context. Nevertheless, it remains an event: the opening "In the thirtieth year of life" is terribly important in locating the *idea* of an event, and in asserting the right to treat an event abstractly. Whether the event was a divorce, the psychological equivalent of divorce from a person or from the idea of love, or something else, we cannot know. At the same time, knowing that the process of affiancing his heart took place at a specified time helps clarify the hurtful and ironic way in which he is free and "it" is bound. Abstract yet personal and even intimate, such definition of the ground between freedom and captivity, as between loving and being pleased, could even be called a kind of confession.

The word "confession," after all, means or once meant something other than a declaration of guilt or revelation of sins. It can signify a personal declaration of belief or conviction. It can mean the formal statement of a creed, and as such it has constituted a literary kind. The traditional and contemporary senses of the word come together on the note of personal conviction, of making your mind known to others in Berryman's sense.

The poems of Frank Bidart share something like that note with "Epigram #1," different as they are in most other ways. Bidart's diction is often "abstract," but in the way that the colloquial speech of the poet's class, place, and time can be abstract. The rhythms, too, are based on the serious, intense speech of the poet and his contemporaries, as Cunningham's rhythms are based on the iambic tradition of Jonson. Bidart's prosody relies on the way line-endings and white space can indicate or heighten the pauses and emphases of conversation. And in structure, too, Bidart often relies on a slowly expanding, inclusive form analogous to speech. If it is necessary to test how a Cunningham epigram makes known the mind, it is necessary to ask what, in Bidart's work, gives the statement the firmness of poetry. The answer, I think, lies in a determination like Cunningham's to pursue a statement beyond or outside such matters as the nominalist tradition, the inclination to wit, or the appeal of the exquisite image.

The title poem of Bidart's book *Golden State* is an address, in ten numbered parts, to the poet's father. The immediate occasion is the father's funeral. Here is part II:

> It's in many ways
> a relief to have you dead.
>
>   I have more money.
> Bakersfield is easier: life isn't so nude,

now that I no longer have to
face you each evening: mother is progressing
beautifully in therapy, I can almost convince myself
a good analyst would have saved you:

for I *need* to believe, as
always, that your pervasive sense of disappointment

proceeded from
trivial desires: but I fear
that beneath the wish to be a movie star,
cowboy, empire builder, all those
cheap desires, lay
radical disaffection
                              from the very possibilities
of human life . . .

Your wishes were too simple:
                              or too complex.

There is an initial shock at reading a poem that bases itself so
genuinely upon the writer's way of speaking, as we can imagine
it: modulating from "progressing beautifully" to "radical disaf-
fection," permitting "cowboy" to fall where it might and "trivial"
to alternate with "cheap." We are not used to poems that actually
base their diction upon a heightened version of the earnest
speech used by the poet's social class. This is not merely the
familiar literary version of speech that poets, in order to be col-
loquial, create from sources like Williams, Hemingway, country
music, and the phrases used by advertising or by teenage infor-
mants. That constructed idiom is "literary" partly because it is
bound to avoid too many phrases that evoke the speech of
people who read or try to make literature; that is, a poet who

undertakes diction like "insight" and "disaffection," contriving to use it along with "bag of money" and "movie star," as naturally as he would in speech, sets out to claim an almost revolutionary freedom.

As with Cunningham's use of abstract diction, such freedom involves limitations and risks. Most obvious is the risk of flatness, which "Golden State" meets by limiting itself to a gravely linear development, a careful adherence to the moral issues. Such a style sacrifices unpredictability; the poem offers revelations, but no surprises of a radical kind. This discipline gives the texture of the writing a firm, vigorous quality; the abstract terms and speaking voice turn out, repeatedly, to have their own, rather investigative, kind of precision. But such poetry depends in a special way upon what it will say about its subject, in the way that we expect of prose. To put it another way, where and what, specifically, is the emotion here?

The desires of the opening lines of the section are for ease of different kinds: "relief," "more money," easiness of life clothed in avoidance or in progress toward health, the nudity of conflict and of yearning almost hidden away. None of this is ironic—very little in "Golden State" is ironic—for the poet does not hold ease, or peace, cheap; and for what it is worth, therapy can be "good." These desires are true not ironically but, characteristically, "in many ways."

In relation to the father, however, that scheme of desired ends becomes wishful thinking. The compromises of progress toward the good and avoidance of evil appear to be wishful thinking, or evasions, before the father's massive unhappiness. The question is, does a craving for some absolute glory or pleasure, beyond the apparent possibilities and compromises of actual life, constitute something infantile and trivial, or something irresistibly heroic, demanding loyalty? For the reasonable, decent-sounding poet, characterized by his careful honesty in the opening lines, the answer seems to lean away from such careful compromise and toward the unreasonable, indecently hungry shapes of desire. In the language of compromise and caution, the poem expresses its own radical impatience with the limits of life. The father's needs were too simple or too complex for any easy survival in the world, and also too simple or too complex to be dismissed in the name of an ideal based upon the limits of the world.

Thus, the element of abstract diction in the writing, like the reliance on definition and statement, has two different effects. On the surface, the effect is an air of dogged sincerity, an almost clinical honesty patterned by the rhythms of a naturalistic voice. In a deeper way, the abstractions do what abstractions always tend to do: they assert the presence or pursuit of an absolute, some value transcending the particulars of experience. Just as Cunningham turns from the experience of marriage toward an idea, or Jonson from the experience of a child toward the idea of the child's soul, one element in these lines turns from the world of experience—therapies and movie stars—toward some impossibly complex (or crude) hunger beyond life.

This is more clear in the tenth and final section of "Golden State":

> When I began this poem,
>   to see myself
> as a piece of history, having a past
> which shapes, and informs, and thus inevitably
> limits—

> at first this seemed sufficient, the beginning of
> freedom ...
> The way to approach freedom
> was to acknowledge necessity:—
> I sensed I had to become not merely
> a speaker, the "eye," but a character ...
>
> And you had to become a character: with a past,
> with a set of internal contradictions and necessities
> which if I could *once* define, would at least
> begin to release us from each other ...
>
> But, of course, no such knowledge is possible;—
> as I touch your photographs, they stare back at me
> with the dazzling, impenetrable, glitter of mere life ...
>
> You stand smiling, at the end of the twenties,
> in a suit, and hat,
> cane and spats, with a collie at your feet,
> happy to be handsome, dashing, elegant:—
>
> and though I cannot connect this image
> with the end of your life, with the defensive
> gnarled would-be cowboy,—
>
> you seem happy at that fact, happy
> to be surprising; unknowable; unpossessable ...
>
> You say it's what you always understood by freedom.

Though he has become unknowable, he speaks. Between the
impenetrable, nominalistic glitter of "mere life" on one side, and
the vast, remote idea of freedom on the other, the dead figure,

for all his grotesque vanity and posturing, embodies an ideal: no matter how corrupt or trivial the circumstances and possibilities of life may be, one can try to live free of them, and that idea of freedom survives the particulars and necessities of life. That is a traditional emotional action for elegy, as *Lycidas* exemplifies.

Because of the snapshot-image of the well-turned-out father, some readers of "Golden State" will think of the possible influence of Robert Lowell's *Life Studies*. Stylistically, however, Lowell's poems often rely upon a series of bitter or ironic incongruities, surprises of contrasted or unexpectedly extended images:

> He still treasured underhand economies,
> but his best friend was his little black *Chevie*,
> garaged like a sacrificial steer
> with gilded hooves,
> yet sensationally sober,
> and with less side than an old dancing pump.

("TERMINAL DAYS AT BEVERLY FARMS")

This grim, unpredictable wandering into invention has the effect of relieving the potential banality or pointlessness of the material; we feel the poet needing the inventive language as a kind of polished shield in which he can regard the father's reflection without being overcome by pity or some other emotion. The rich catalogue of details and figures supplies a varied, many-colored background; against that background of nearly random colors, the plainness of closing lines like "I feel awful" can stand out.

The method of Bidart's "Golden State" is quite different. Most biography is potentially banal or pointless, a circumstance "Golden State" meets with the stylistic opposite of Lowell's nervously varied surface texture. Instead, we have the speaking voice described above, and the implied promise to penetrate the subject, however "unpoetic" it may seem at times. If that commitment and its voice are—like Cunningham's pentameter abstractions—confining, they are also liberating.

II. Ammons

From the beginning, some of the most exciting, overwhelming moments in the modernist tradition have come when a poet breaks through into the kind of prose freedom and prose inclusiveness I have tried to suggest with words like "discourse" and "discursive." The freedom and scope of speech may convey the idea better than those of prose, if by speech we mean not its idiom, but its way of moving, inquiring, expanding. This generosity of movement, in modern poetry, is peculiarly affecting. I have in mind a range of passages in which the dull plains of description or the exactions of the "image" are not abandoned, but transcended: the poet claims the right to make an interesting remark or to speak of profundities, with all of the liberty given to the newspaper editorial, a conversation, a philosopher, or any speaker whatever.

Because of the philosophical and emotional background of modernist techniques, because of the techniques themselves, and because the anti-verbal prejudice is transcended, such passages are exhilarating: the breezy lines of Williams when he seems to build his poem upon an interesting remark ("It's the anarchy of poverty/ delights me"); Eliot's dark, abstract set-speech on History in "Gerontion"; the autobiographical, passionate moralizing of Canto LXXXIII ("Here error is all in the not done,/ all in the diffidence that faltered"). All of these are especially moving to us because the language has emerged through the underlying confines of description, mastering description and going beyond it to words as a means of life.

A fine example of what I mean, and for many readers perhaps a supreme example, is Stevens's "Sunday Morning." Earlier, I have discussed "The Snow Man" as a superb poem posing the terms of the nominalist-realist dilemma: the words, ideas, and feelings that might seem real to a human observer are "not there" in a landscape; yet except for those nominal words, ideas, and feelings we have no way of observing the flow of particulars or "nothing" that *is* there. If "The Snow Man" demonstrates how profoundly that philosophical quandary can be felt, "Sunday Morning" demonstrates how deeply we respond to a transcendence of the quandary.

The poem's remarkable blending of sensory detail and intellectual definition, natural image and abstract term, has often been pointed out by critics, especially in regard to the last sections. Consider, too, the third section, which gives a kind of lightning-summary of the anthropological history of religion:

> Jove in the clouds had his inhuman birth.
> No mother suckled him, no sweet land gave
> Large-mannered motions to his mythy mind.
> He moved among us, as a muttering king,
> Magnificent, would move among his hinds,

Until our blood, commingling, virginal,
With heaven, brought such requital to desire
The very hinds discerned it, in a star.
Shall our blood fail? Or shall it come to be
The blood of paradise? And shall the earth
Seem all of paradise that we shall know?
The sky will be much friendlier then than now,
A part of labor and a part of pain,
And next in glory to enduring love,
Not this dividing and indifferent blue.

This is the history, not only of religion's past, but of its future, too. And one reason it moves us so, I think, is that we feel the poet's language expanding to the full reach of its grand style, to a breadth of predication, as it pushes upward from the solidness of a created natural world of sky, weather, birds. That movement toward intellectual speculation, Stevens convinces us, in some way parallels the historical motion he dares to summarize: an idea of god as remote from earth and the human mind changes to an idea of god as partly human—and, finally, to an idea of divinity that does not "fail" while becoming wholly human and of the earth. Poetry itself, we feel as we read "Sunday Morning," can move from mythology to metaphorical imagery to, finally, a sublimely direct relationship between experience and words. Stevens overcomes our doubts of such a relationship by force: the force of his Wordsworthian grand style, and of his piercing natural images.

I have referred to an "anti-verbal prejudice." Although earlier sections of this book help justify the use of such a phrase, this is a suitable point for offering some evidence that such a prejudice exists, and that it is also possible to find related ideas like "the effacement of the poet," and in far from negligible writing. The first example is from critical prose, an essay on "The New Surrealism":

> The poem proceeds by needle-thrusts of imagery. . . . There is a kind of anonymity in the tone, as if the images emerged without a voice, from out of the language itself. This is a touchstone of the pure surrealist text, which avoids giving any sense of personality, since what is being written belongs to the flow of pure chance, not to the needs and feelings of a "self." . . . [T]he poet may be telling us that his poems are written by nobody; that they come from no place, and mean nothing.[2]

I feel that the title of the essay, and its subject, are important to mention, because the poems in question are in some ways a new departure, by fairly young writers; and the ideas of anonymity and non-predication are matters I have tried to trace back as far as the "Ode to a Nightingale." In the quotation, the phrase "from out of the language itself" might seem to contradict the idea of an anti-verbal bias; however, "language" in the quotation is not a means for predicating concepts or making statements about experience. Rather, the word is used as part of a reification (to use a fancy word) of language itself; the "language itself" is there only to "mean nothing." At least according to the theory defined by this prose quotation, the "New Surrealism," whatever else it does, does not attack the barriers between consciousness and nature that Stevens seems to force through.

My second and more complex example, which leads back eventually to the ambitions of "Sunday Morning," is from A. R. Ammons's poem "Motion," which begins:

The word is
not the thing:
is
a construction of,
a tag for,
the thing: the
word in no way resembles
the thing, except
as sound
resembles,
as in whirr,
sound:
the relation
between what this
as words
is
and what is
is tenuous: we
agree upon
this as the net to
cast on what
is: the finger
to point with: the
method of
distinguishing,
defining, limiting:

Here, language is not utterly reified; it is understood as being, largely, a defining and distinguishing gesture of the mind, isolating parts of reality. But insofar as it is such a defining gesture, "the word" in this poem has no reality, is no part of "what is." That, by definition, is the nominalist view of language; as general categories, words are arbitrary and unreal, however convenient. The poem suggests that words can be a part of "what is"—or rather can manage to *resemble* "what is"—only to the extent that they are particulars: that is, in their sound. "Motion" goes on to extend this idea logically from words to poems as a whole:

> poems
> are fingers, methods,
> nets,
> not what is or was:
> but the music
> in poems
> is different,
> points to nothing,
> traps no
> realities, takes
> no game, but
> by the motion of
> its motion
> resembles
> what, moving, is—
> the wind
> underleaf white against
> the tree.

The poem is extraordinary in that it presents a view of language that is lucid, rigorously thought out, and hard to disagree with. (Although Ammons has elaborated this position in later poems, I believe that he has not fundamentally changed it.) To that extent the poem succeeds in discoursing, without the suasion of a grand style, about its materials, forcefully arguing—the word seems just—that the words of a poem have two distinct aspects; and, the aspect that defines or captures reality is precisely the one that fails to "resemble" reality, which is particular and fluid.

To summarize: Stevens in "Sunday Morning" imagines a kind of harmony or rapprochement between the conceptions created by the human mind and the particulars of the world, and he makes a poetic style that makes such a divine partnership credible, by the way it mingles the senses and the sense of the mind. Ammons in "Motion" presents the division as absolute and so, implicitly, more problematical for the poet, since the parts of his medium that most "trap" reality are least like it, and vice versa.

The division of essential nature between words and reality is an especially difficult issue for this particular poet, who has a bent toward abstraction, toward authenticating abstraction as an activity, and toward keeping his predicating, assertive self in the poem. All of those inclinations conflict with the impersonal, yielding method and conception reflected by Ammons's poem "Poetics," which ends with these lines, logically consistent with the ideas of "Motion":

> not so much looking for the shape
> as being available
> to any shape that may be

summoning itself
through me
from the self not mine but ours.

This passivity and self-effacement also underlie Ammons's well-known poem "Corson's Inlet," which begins on the page after "Motion" in the *Collected Poems*. Together, I think these poems help explain the strange, unmistakable style of Ammons. His work is based upon a clear, concentrated meditation of the problem that I have made central to this book. The result is a difficult marriage of poetics or epistemology with natural description: the fluid landscape and the poet's repeated definition of his own role in relation to that flux. The style that strives to resolve these demands is strained in various directions, with an oddly garrulous reliance upon claims and disclaimers. The concluding stanzas of "Corson's Inlet," for example, comprise an awkwardly argumentative, definitive, self-conscious protest against argument, definitiveness and unwillingness "to go along, to accept/ the becoming/ thought":

orders as summaries, as outcomes of actions override
or in some way result, not predictably (seeing me gain
the top of a dune,
the swallows
could take flight—some other fields of bayberry
        could enter fall
        berryless) and there is serenity:

                no arranged terror: no forcing of image, plan,
or thought:
no propaganda, no humbling of reality to precept:

THE DISCURSIVE ASPECT OF POETRY 193

terror pervades but is not arranged, all possibilities
of escape open: no route shut, except in
the sudden loss of all routes:

The strained, nearly pinched quality of the idiom ("still around,"
"there is serenity," "widening scope") goes oddly with the self-
praise or self-admonishment in the language of literary criti-
cism: "I . . . will not run to that easy victory" or "finality of vi-
sion." In the presence of so much strain, it is hard to credit either
the joy or the capitalization of "Scope" in the phrase "enjoying
the freedom that/ Scope eludes my grasp"; and the phrase is,
along with the rest of the final five lines, contingent upon the
line "I will try." This tentative, doubting quality—an "enlarging"
and difficult resolve simply to "try"—characterizes Ammons's
most memorable work, strangely as it does conflict with the
assertive, proscriptive tone of "no forcing," "will not run," and
"there is no finality": a largely negative definitiveness. Am-
mons's more prophetic, Romantically affirmative poems are
both fewer and less convincing—like "The City Limits," in

which the abundance of natural "radiance" falls on the accepting earth around one until:

> the dark
> work of the deepest cells is of a tune with May bushes
> and fear lit by the breadth of such calmly turns to praise.

If fear ever turns "calmly" to anything, being "of a tune with May bushes" is a lamely rhetorical motive for such turning, especially given the sinister, cancerous implications of "the dark work of the deepest cells." Moreover, it is the "breadth" of the natural world itself, and its radiance, which kindle fear. In "Corson's Inlet," the "grasps of disorder" as a goal, the pervasive terror, and the unpredictable, uncontrolled appearance of serenity carry more conviction than the "praise" of "The City Limits." The reason, I think, is that in "Corson's Inlet" Ammons's voice conveys the difficulty and tentativeness of its own role in the world, a role within which neither praise nor vision can come with finality or for long.

Perhaps more than any other contemporary poet, Ammons displays a consistent, explicit, intelligent taking up of the themes and problems I have tried to present as central to the modernist tradition. He takes up the implications of the great poetic subject I have exemplified by citing the "Ode to a Nightingale," "The Most of It," "The Term," and "The Snow Man"; it is even possible to argue that he brings to that subject a discursive style. So it is essential for me to explain why I find something dull and strained in his work, for all its accomplishments. Underlying that particular question is the larger question of how gravely limiting the traditional problem at stake must be for contemporary poetry.

The problem can be summarized as a need to find language for presenting the role of a conscious soul in an unconscious world; the terms, of course, vary historically and from individual to individual. "Sunday Morning" suggests that for a human being "divinity must live within herself," finding correspondences in the natural world for internal passions—

> unsubdued
> Elations when the forest blooms; gusty
> Emotions on wet roads on autumn nights;
> All pleasures and all pains, remembering
> The bough of summer and the winter branch.

The unconscious natural world provides "destined" comparisons, figures of speech, terms or "measures" for the conscious soul and its actions. Through a blank-verse style that is a sort of rich distillation of Wordsworth's, Stevens makes this arrangement seem rich and promising, a spiritual correspondence dwelling in the poetic mind. The style is grand, and indeed implies a grandly hieratic role for the poet and his language, which becomes a religious medium.

The characteristic manner of Ammons seems at moments similarly grand, but with odd catches or mutterings, an undertone of uncertainty and misgiving that becomes explicit in the following poem:

Plunder

I have appropriated the windy twittering of aspen leaves
into language, stealing something from reality like a
silverness: drop-scapes of ice from peak sheers:

much of the rise in brooks over slow-rolled glacial stones:
the loop of reeds over the shallow's edge when birds
feed on the rafts of algae: I have taken right out of the

air the clear streaks of bird music and held them in my
head like shifts of sculptured glint: I have sent language
through the mud roils of a racoon's paws like a net,

netting the roils: made my own use of a downwind's
urgency on a downward stream: held with a large scape
of numbness the black distance upstream to the
    mountains

flashing and bursting: meanwhile, everything else, frog,
fish, bear, gnat has turned in its provinces and made off
with its uses: my mind's indicted by all I've taken.

A poem like this depends upon great sharpness of physical de-
tail, and "Plunder" is convincingly vivid in many of its natural
images, particularly in the second stanza: the loop of the reeds,
the algae in abundant rafts. But this adept descriptive writing,
which is part of the poem's subject, is halted or made jagged by
what seems a deliberate flatting: the limping phrases "like a/
silverness," "like shifts of sculptured glint" and "held with a
large scape/ of numbness." These mumbled similes and
"-nesses" act as protestations of how difficult and oblique a pro-
cess this plundering-by-language is, for the poet. On the one
hand, there is the assertion of bardic power, and on the other
hand, the poet doubts the integrity of what he does when he
tries to find likenesses for the glitter of reality. The doubt is lit-
eral, it is implicit in the halted style, and it is explicit in the con-
clusion of the poem: the "appropriating" and "stealing" that

seem to indicate the poet's authority and subtlety in the first stanza become literal transgressions by the last line.

As a result, the tone and scope of "Plunder" are peculiar; it appears that personally, the poet praises himself, while philosophically, he throws literal, grave misgivings upon what he has done with his mind and his language. However, I think that the repeated presence of the note of bardic assertion in Ammons's work is no mere disorganization or accident of personality. That sometimes combative, intrusive presence is, as I have pointed out, somewhat paradoxical in view of the "yielding" advocated in "Corson's Inlet," the "self not mine." Yet it is an inevitable presence given the assumptions and bases of these poems.

That is, Ammons believes in abstraction, he has no desire to sink into pure description or to be a nature poet, and yet he also believes deeply that the mind and its essential tool—the net or method of words—are indicted by the flux of reality. And so, between the alternatives of description and what might be called Romantic epistemology—an obsessive redefinition of the poet's relationship to natural reality—we also have the mediating presence of bardic self-assertion. The bardic note, in a way, is not an emotion itself, but rather a way of holding together other, conflicting emotions. To some extent, it performs the same role as the mellowly oracular grand style of "Sunday Morning."

Thus, Stevens discourses about the largest of abstract questions while evoking the natural world, and all the time implies—but never states—a central role for the poet as a spiritual model. Ammons, conversely, must discourse explicitly about the role of the poet in order to make his way, by apology and explanation, toward philosophical questions and the natural world. "Corson's Inlet" is largely an account of the walks on which the poet discovers the sources, and the limits, of his poems; this procedure, and what might seem a boastful or self-obsessed personal mode, are in fact corollaries of Romantic epistemology: the perpetual mending and inspection of the net of language.

The limits of such material and such a style are severe; the poet cannot in good faith go very far from natural phenomena, and his own relation to reality. These limitations are reflected stylistically in the movement and diction of a poem like "Plunder." In diction, the ambivalence appears in semi-ironic reclamations of Romantic vocabulary: "twittering," "flashing and bursting," "provinces." In movement from part to part, the strings of repeated colons suggest a conflict between the stationary or simultaneous and the developing or sequential; each part explains every other part, with a minimum of the consecutive structuring in which part rests on part as in a building or a tree. This closeless structure is the contrary of Stevens's elaborately organized periods, and the contrary of the kind of progress I mean by the word "discursive." Ammons makes very much the same point himself, using the similar word "disquisition":

> (disquisition is sesquipedalian pedestrianism, tidying up
>   the loose bits, but altogether missing the import of the
>   impetus):
> a center's absolute, if relative: but every point in
>   spacetimematter's
>
> a center: reality is abob with centers: indeed, there is
>   nothing but centers:

("ESSAY ON POETICS")

Entirely as I disagree with this passage, insofar as it calls for a kind of poetry, or decries one, I think that it sets the terms of the matter accurately. The passage itself illustrates the awkwardness with which Ammons must approach the chore of disquisition: the strained jocularity of the wordplays and chattiness, the impatient alliterations, the slightly false slang and breeziness, all express a certain embarrassment with the task at hand. The more congenial style and material of "Plunder" represent an honorable and masterful kind of poetry, moving within its narrow spectrum. But the human limits—the *social* limits, the conversational limits—of Romantic epistemology suggest a diminishing of poetry's scope, if not a dead end. The limits and pressures I have described produce the style that, reading Ammons, I find myself calling "dull," pinched, hard to read with absorption despite my other response of admiration.

III. McMichael's "Itinerary"

Our difference from the rest of nature is a profound subject; but it is not the only subject, however much an awareness of it has affected the way we see and the way we use words. Can that subject be dealt with or included while not sacrificing the breadth of our human concerns? Another way of putting the question is to ask whether the subject can be dealt with in a style of discourse something like the ones I have admired in Bidart and Cunningham. I would like to quote an extended passage from James McMichael's extraordinary long poem "Itinerary," a poem that tours through the minds and voices of various American speakers as we move eastward across the continent and back in history. Although a kind of troubled love affair with

the landscape provides one essential strand in "Itinerary," Mc-
Michael does not explore the theme with anything like the ob-
sessive complexity of Ammons. Rather, it is as though McMi-
chael, the younger poet, takes the division between mind and
nature as one more traditional theme, a part of cultural history
within him along with Christianity, mythology, courtly love,
the history of his country. These concerns are disposed and de-
veloped in an easily discursive manner: a readable, well-
proportioned quality. "Itinerary" is not as intricate a meditation
on the mind-nature division as "Corson's Inlet," let alone "Sun-
day Morning"; but it does include that theme, and the kinds of
attractive poetic language that grow from that theme, within a
large world of its own materials. Instead of the complex episte-
mology of "Corson's Inlet," we have a complex world of human
affairs, of which the American wilderness is one.

This passage is from near the end of "Itinerary," at the Vir-
ginia coast of colonial times:

> We perceive our appetites to mend,
> and though we have to drink only what
> Adam had in Paradise, that stream of life
> runs cool and peaceably in our veins.
> The days are hard. Our slumbers sweeten, and
> if we ever dream of women they are kind.
> I delight to see the banks of the Inlet
> adorned with myrtle, yet it must be owned
> that, sacred to Venus though it be, this plant
> grows commonly in very dirty soil.
> Norfolk has most the air of a town
> of any in Virginia. There are now

riding at her wharves near 20 brigantines.
The trade hither is engrossed by those
saints of New England who every week
carry off a pretty deal of tobacco.
I have found that after my devotions
a walk in the garden can do much
to fill my heart with clear obedience.
I repair me there that I might think
deeply of the earth and how it will be
all too soon my resting-place. For I am told
to fear such things as bring me to ill terms,
told of those who seek congress with the earth
that they shall have her in their time forever.
That her places sing their love-songs for no man.
That I am not the suitor whose betrothed
awaits him, but some unwelcome third
with God alone her lover. And yet I would
look upon such country as will show me
nature undressed, the strata of the land,
her lays and beds and all her privacies.
For my wonder tells me I should be
promiscuous, should learn by all the
laws of bodies and by where they are
the joyful news out of the new found land.

In part, the historical voice gives McMichael a borrowed poise
and spaciousness. But the words and emotions belong to the
poet, not to a character or series of characters, and the colonial
voice here is not merely a means toward a plausible style; his-
tory is essential to the poem's action. "Itinerary" begins in the

twentieth century and on the Western plains, moving as speakers shift imperceptibly toward the east and the eighteenth century. Perhaps I should say "the speaker shifts," for there are no distinct transitions, and all of the speakers are also the poet: his "sources," in several senses. The action, I think, is the discovery that meditation of the human past and of the natural terrain are inseparable, and that together they are the measures of the poet's soul. To reach the lines I have quoted is to reenact McMichael's historical understanding of nature and its attractions—and, his understanding of the fear

> That her places sing their love-songs for no man.
> That I am not the suitor whose betrothed
> awaits him, but some unwelcome third
> with God alone her lover.

The harmonized elements of sexuality, Christianity, mythology here are not part of a separate "speaker," but aspects of the poet's own love for the natural world; he discovers that complex, troubled love within himself and within his tradition, and demonstrates it as Tennyson demonstrated it in "Tithonus."

The historical journey allows the poem to explore the manifold relationship between the landscape and the plundering mind, not simply as an obsession in itself, but as it is related to the rest of life: patriotism, sexual desire, mortality, all of which are never far from "Itinerary's" voice. In the quoted passage, the matter-of-fact element in the language—"dirty soil," "a pretty deal of tobacco"—subsists easily along with the increasing grandness of the passage, as the poem changes gradually toward blank verse. The style, in other words, proves able to cover considerable ground, with an effect of being compact and leisurely at once. I have implicitly defended the archaism of this passage by suggesting that the historical materials come from inside the poet. One proof of that is the quality of breadth, the sense that the poet can put in and make natural whatever seems pertinent to him. (For instance, the passage I have quoted incorporates transformed quotations, not only from William Byrd and Cotton Mather, but from Simone Weil as well.) The style seems to manage that breadth while keeping its balance: "Those who seek congress with the earth" and those who admonish them are both included, with a measure of sympathetic understanding. Both the balance and the inclusiveness are exemplified by another, slightly earlier passage:

> There fell a sort of Scots mist all the way.
> I have learned how rattlesnakes take a squirrel.
> They ogle the poor beast til by force of charm
> it falls down stupified and senseless.
> The snake approaches it and moistens first
> one ear and then the other with his spawl,
> making the head all slippen. When that is done
> he draws this member into his mouth,
> and after it, by casual degrees,
> all the rest of the body.

And then on to a new subject. The charm of the passage for me is in the way the detachment, the absence of hysteria ("poor beast," "this member") does not sacrifice any of the vivid awfulness: a brief example of "promiscuous wonder." If the passage is a set piece, it is an extremely deft, agreeable one.

As the snake-passage may suggest, "Itinerary" is partly given over to description—too much of it, I think, especially in the earlier, twentieth-century, and Western passages. But even the description has a firm, confident simplicity; here are the poem's opening lines:

> The farmhouses north of Driggs,
> silos for miles along the road saying
> BUTLER or SIOUX. The light saying
> rain coming on, the wind not up yet,
> animals waiting as the front hits
> everything on the high flats, hailstones
> bouncing like rabbits under the sage.
> Nothing running off. Creeks clear.
> The river itself a shallow, straight
> shoot to the north, its rocks mossy,
> slick above the few deep pockets.

It may be significant that the poem is more reportorial, and perhaps too long, in its earlier, modern-idiom passages, reaching its full depth in the later, historical passages: as though the measured archaism were a release of some kind. But the main point is that the poem includes the nominalist dilemma as one historical part of its sensibility among others, like the "God" who is alone nature's lover; in a way, that inclusion may be the poem's subject.

As another such "inclusion," "Itinerary" contains theological or Puritan elements, which are played against erotic ones. In part, these terms raise again the ambivalence about nature's expanse expressed by the "Ode to a Nightingale": to seek "congress with the earth" can mean a sodlike death of the conscious soul, or it can mean a vision into creation, the joyful news of its parts and unities. "Itinerary" deals with this material in a way that is not formulaic: it is not simply that the Puritan element in the poem's voice stands for the earth as an emblem of death and "ill terms" while the erotic element stands for joy in the love of nature. Rather, it is part of the Puritan impulse to repair to the garden and the earth, reading the divine hand in earth's "privacies and lays"; and, the erotic imagery contributes toward the despairing fear that the wilderness means only death:

> That her places sing their love-songs for no man.
> That I am not the suitor whose betrothed
> awaits him, but some unwelcome third
> with God alone her lover.

The complexity that makes all of these viewpoints part of a single surface is reflected by the poem's humanistic sense of people, and groups of people—comic shadings like the communal dreams of kind women, or the saints of New England with their pretty deal of tobacco. Like the poise of the snake-squirrel episode, this humane or social element in "Itinerary" is part of what I mean when I say that McMichael has a subject of his own apart from the epistemology that seems to dominate "Corson's Inlet," which must call for

> no forcing of image, plan
> or thought:
> no propaganda, no humbling of reality to precept.

In a way, this problem is a dead issue for McMichael, whose poem seems to represent a truce between reality and precept. It is as though Ammons is in a deep way earlier in the tradition, and still bound to write propaganda against the dangers of propaganda and "forcing of image."

I have argued that McMichael in "Itinerary" writes in a way that goes freely and discursively to the center of its subject, a center involving the anti-verbal, anti-discursive roots of his tradition. That view of "Itinerary" is supported by the fact that he has written poems that undertake far different kinds of experience, writing in a way comparable to the openness and plainness I have pointed out in the widely varying styles of Bidart and Cunningham. Here is McMichael on marital estrangement, a particular marital estrangement:

Lady Good

It had to be said about her
That she was good, got better still,
And that when he left her, or died,
Or did whatever worse he could
Do to her, that she took it on;
Took on not what he did to her
But what it did to him to do it.

The risks and virtues of this method—personal utterance, plain rhetoric, abstract definition and vocabulary—are clear. One is reminded of the way Cunningham has introduced one of his poems, saying that he likes it because of the regular meter, abstract diction, the absence of images, metaphors, or paradoxes, its unambiguity, and so forth. But McMichael's spirit in this poem is not one of teasing or challenging received ideas, or aggressively unfashionable. The poem defines a woman's generosity and the painful drawbacks of the generosity with remarkable delicacy and firmness. The poem is a statement, made in the tone of a human being speaking of and to human beings, with all of the excitement of poetry.

IV. Poetic Dictions and Prose Virtues

Stylistically, much of what I have said about the discursive aspect of poetry may come down to a call for "the prose virtues," as they are sometimes called. Colorless and reactionary though such a position may seem, it is worth taking up. Pound made the often-quoted assertion that poetry atrophies when it gets too far from music—observing, also, that poetry must be at least as well-written as prose. What happens to poetry when it gets too far from prose, and the prose virtues? If the plural is analyzed, the virtues turn out to be a drab, unglamorous group, including perhaps Clarity, Flexibility, Efficiency, Cohesiveness ... a puritanical assortment of shrews. They do not as a rule appear in blurbs. And yet when they are courted by those who understand them—William Carlos Williams and Elizabeth Bishop would be examples—the Prose Virtues are transformed from a supporting chorus to the performers of virtuoso marvels. They can become not merely the poem's minimum requirement, but the poetic essence.

One of the most contemporary strains in contemporary poetry is often interior, submerged, free-playing, elusive, more fresh than earnest, more eager to surprise than to tell. The "surrealist" diction associated with such writing sometimes suggests, not a realm beyond surface reality, but a *particular* reality, hermetically primitive, based on a new poetic diction: "breath," "snow," "future," "blood," "silence," "eats," "water," and most of all "light" doing the wildly unexpected. On the one hand, some poetic diction or other may be inescapable even for the greatest masters. But on the other hand, poets have been known, historically, to strangle their work on gobbets of poetic diction; when poetry gets too far from prose, it may be in danger of choking itself on a thick, rich handful of words.

In one recent book of poems,[3] which contains all of the words listed above, light "drills" into eyes "like a stream of liquid beads"; a "little loaf of light" rises "in the sea's dark pan"; a "shard of light," in one of the run-on images that characterize all poetic dictions everywhere, is "in the shape of an island from which dogs are leaping into the water"—but then, the poet muses, "or maybe the light implodes"; there appear "eels of shy light"; another person must "go the rest of the way/ by eating the light." The blank, simple substances—snow, water, air—create a world where "silence" reigns and "eating" is the main, monumental process: "we eat our way through grief and make it richer." The monumental quality of these word-denying images, and the potential exquisiteness of surrealism, are balanced by banal, contemporary objects: people lie down in "snow sandwiches"; "Sleep is my radio and/ all its news is true." This is a kind of one-of-the-guys surrealism.

The purpose of calling attention to such writing is not simply to proscribe figurative language and figurative structures that go beyond the surfaces of life, in the surrealist mode. What must be pointed out is the horrible ease with which a stylish rhetoric can lead poetry unconsciously to abandon life itself.

It also must be pointed out that poems that seem wildly unpredictable and resourceful sometimes are bound by a fairly narrow poetic diction, and the view of reality and language that diction implies. For example, James Tate's poem "The Wheelchair Butterfly" presents a spectacular range of images in the classic surrealist manner, beginning:

> O sleepy city of reeling wheelchairs
> Where a mouse can commit suicide.

It can be difficult to give such a poem a structure or movement from beginning to end, and Tate seems to respond to that problem by alluding to the diction I have been discussing; "The Wheelchair Butterfly" ends:

> Honeysuckle says: I thought I could swim.

> The mayor is urinating on the wrong side
> of the street! A dandelion sets off sparks:
> beware your hair is locked!

> Beware the trumpet wants a glass of water!
> Beware a velvet tabernacle!

> Beware the Warden of Light has married
> an old piece of string!

On a somewhat higher level of writing, the piece of string balances "Light" as the "sandwiches" balance the "snow." The main point is that Tate resolves his poem partly by including water and light, the "poetic" words that seem to deepen the unpredictable shimmer of the language. (Since "The Wheelchair Butterfly" is the last poem in *The Norton Anthology of Modern Poetry*, it is interesting to note that the last four lines in that volume contain two of the words that seem to constitute a current, identifiable poetic diction.)

A prevalent diction or manner can be practiced well or ill, and will tend to reflect certain general concerns or senses of experience. The diction and manner I am talking about stem from the fact that certain contemporary poets have devised ways of writing that go remarkably far toward embodying, in language, a host of reservations about language, human reason, and their holds on life. For instance, W. S. Merwin's poem "Whenever I Go There," which I have discussed in chapter III, part IV, moves in a resolutely elliptical way from image to atomistic image, finally reaching a kind of generalization-against-generalizing:

> Today belongs to few and tomorrow to no one

As I have said earlier, this poem presents a style well suited to a certain deeply skeptical or limiting vision of the poetic imagination and its place in the world. Perception is more to be trusted than reflection, former ideas are obstacles, and the large, blank, irreducible phenomena are the truest incarnations of reality. But because the style is so distinctly identifiable, it is liable to be taken, or taken over, as a kind of stylistic lingua franca, divorced from the philosophical questions or personal inclinations that give the style its coherence and integrity.

Merwin is not the only origin for the style, but his work has certainly contributed to its amalgam of special words and images. It is not hard to find examples that tend to confirm my suggestion that these words and images are related to ideas about speech—as in this passage, the last stanza of Charles Wright's poem "Dog Creek Mainline":

The tongue is a white water.
In its slick ceremonies the light
Gathers, and is refracted, and moves
Outward, over the lips,
Over the dry skin of the world.
The tongue is a white water.

Examples of this diction will vary considerably in their char-
acter and quality. In general, the more any style is taken for
granted, the more abusive the practice of it can become.
Somewhere, on some campus in America, a young poet is
writing a sentence with all or nearly all of the totemic words,
something like:

The silence of my
blood eats light like the
breath of future water,

which I have composed in less time than it takes to type, and
which is the contemporary version of, say:

The fiery blossoms fading in the twilight,

and while it remains true that "light" and "snow" and "eating"
and "breath" can embody significant ideas, so too can "blos-
som" and "twilight"; and poetic diction is poetic diction, an
automatic ornament whether it steals its glitter from the sur-
faces of Tennyson or from those of more contemporary poets.

Thus, however much we may weary of poems in which people
go to sleep in sandwiches made with snow, or in which they wear
pants carved out of silence, the objection is not to the language
of surrealism or the subject of silence. The surrealist enterprise

can reveal unsuspected, essential parts of the invisible web of thoughts covering the world. (Usually, this revelation depends upon a rather proselike, sensible context or frame.) And silence, or disengagement from life, is a profound subject. For an instance of how surrealist, or at least somewhat "irrational" images can make a passage work, consider James Wright's "Two Poems about President Harding." Wright expresses an elegiac, merciful sympathy for his innocent, good-looking, for-a-while-lucky subject: a fairly nice man doomed to live in contemptuous, popular memory as a joke, and not without justice. The demands on our respect made by Harding's beery generosity, his pride and unreflective "beauty," could not have been made clear by more direct, unironic, "rational" figurative language. Here are the last lines of the first Harding-poem, "His Death":

> Tonight,
> The cancerous ghosts of old con men
> Shed their leaves.
> For a proud man,
> Lost between the turnpike near Cleveland
> And the chiropractors' signs looming among dead
>   mulberry trees,
> There is no place left to go
> But home.
>
> "Warren lacks mentality," one of his friends said.
>
> Yet he was beautiful, he was the snowfall
> Turned to white stallions standing still
> Under dark elm trees.
> He died in public. He claimed the secret right
> To be ashamed.

Assuming that there is some truth in any widely felt admiration, the horses evoke what was admirable in the small-town, small-time America of Harding, as the ghosts of old con men evoke the shabbiness and despair. I think that the poem suggests, convincingly, that any one of us might be first "vaguely stunned" like some stupid mammal by the good luck that recognizes one's minor virtues—and then in that stunned state be clobbered for our major failings. The snowfall and its beautiful illusions "are" the poet's sympathy with that fate in Harding: the silence, privacy, and exposure.

For an instance of how silence, in the sense of removal from life, can be treated as a profound subject, I would like to quote from a poem by Richard Schramm, whose first volume of poems is called *Rooted in Silence*. One of Schramm's recurrent subjects is the way the mind moves between the unreachable, obsessive roots of silence and the other demands of life, primarily other people. The silence is defined in "Still Water at Midnight," where the scene is a mountain campsite on the night after a long climb, with other people sleeping on beds of bracken at the speaker's back. He watches the light and stillness on the lake's surface; he imagines touching that surface lightly with his spread hand, changing it, and recalls walking all day "outside others." Then, in the complex final image he turns further away from the companions, toward silence, and then in a way returns:

> On beds of bracken
> People are sleeping and away
>
> by themselves
> pack animals are soaring in the dark.
> By now I have forgotten how I came,

the words I used to convince myself
over the mountains, keep back from
still water, break out of shadow
and carry the sun again

on my eyelid
too full to lift up or by brushing
shake out the salt from my eyes.
All day I have walked outside others
hearing things I grew up with fall
in the softness of just-used air.
As well as I know this place

I know these people
at my back, can see their words
settling down like flakes of dust,
can feel them closing after me
a field of grasses left behind.
I stand up on torn muscles
crackling the stillness to throw

off my clothes
and leap in the soundless skein
of light burning into my flesh
as I plummet in starlight icing
my eyes, touch bottom, and rise
into splintering air breaking breath
in the frost fire falling around me.

To explain why the subject of solitude seems realized here, and
why the light, water, and breath are not mere conventions, I
must appeal to the prose virtues. The release of "breaking

breath" is a successfully hovering modifier, describing what "I" do and, on a secondary level, also acknowledging the way that "air" reclaims the diver. The light caught by the dark water's breakable surface is real light, cast by the actual stars and moon; and it is also the hurtful, bracing medium that attracts the poet away from the warm, word-bound landscape of human relations. That is the landscape to which the diver must return. The first stanza of "Still Water at Midnight" prepares for that inevitable return:

> If I touch it
> I know everything will alter
> even if lightly I lay my hand
> a water-strider on star shine,
> this stillness breathing on my skin
> will startle, shift away from me
> and scatter just beyond my reach.

The pure, silent light of the natural world is essentially "beyond reach," always "altered" by consciousness. Because the silent blank is made physically convincing, and because its "unreachable" quality is realized, I am also convinced of the emotional presence of that silence—water, light, star-shine, and air. "Still Water at Midnight" is not a great poem, but it succeeds in finding an intellectual and emotional reality in some of the means and materials of its time.

V. Final Remarks

It is hard to know how to close this book, with its subject that recedes into the future. I have tried to write not a guidebook but a traveler's essay, offering not a map but a template or overlay, and as a result there can be no absolute resolution or completion. However, here are some summarizing quotations that seem relevant to at least one task of poetry that has concerned me: to deal both with the inert circumstances of the world and the spirit's hunger for true speech.

First, from the first contemporary poem I can remember reading, Allen Ginsberg's address to the shade of Whitman, "A Supermarket in California":

> Will we stroll dreaming of the lost America of love past blue automobiles in driveways, home to our silent cottage?
>
> Ah, dear father, graybeard, lonely old courage-teacher, what America did you have when Charon quit poling his ferry and you got out on a smoking bank and stood watching the boat disappear on the black waters of Lethe?

Ginsberg has gone to the garish, humble temple of material abundance as part of a random but urgent search, "in my hungry fatigue, and shopping for images . . . dreaming of your enumerations." "Shopping for images" among the blue cars, the watermelons and pork chops, Ginsberg is courting some muse or inspiration to animate the cold but attractive things and circumstances of his home terrain. That shopping for significance, for something worth enumerating, is propelled by Ginsberg's personality, a personality of amazing energy even in its gloomy loneliness. The spiritual value he craves and questions is the lost or dead idea of America as a religion. Though oblivion and forgetfulness seem to overwhelm any enumerated image of Amer-

ica in the poem, the bardic personality, of Whitman and Gins-
berg, survives as a moving ideal. A beautiful, broody comedy
transforms a theme like that of "The Waste Land": the failure of
culture to sustain an individual personality amid a world of
things. Between those rather fondly observed things, and the
vague craving for his impossible America, Ginsberg's odd qual-
ity of speech—a zestful self-pity—is an act of memory, memo-
rializing both Whitman and the traditional language of the
poem's closing lines. The inertness of the things in the "neon
fruit supermarket" is overcome by the force that speaks its er-
ratic way toward Charon and Lethe.

The poem uses speech and personality to cure its forlorn di-
lemma in a way that reminds me of George Gascoigne, in "Dan
Bartholomew's Dolorous Discourses," weeping and sweating,
in the bath, over his skinny shanks and his broken heart:

> *Then farewell faith, thou art no woman's fere.**
> And with that word I stay my tongue in time;
> With rolling eyes I look about each where
> Lest any man should hear my raving rime.
> And all in rage, enraged as I am,
> I take my sheet, my slippers, and my gown,
> And in the Bath from whence I late but came,
> I cast myself in dolors there to drown.
> There all alone I can myself convey
> Into some corner where I sit unseen,
> And to myself, there naked, can I say:
> Behold these brawn-fallen arms which once have been
> Both large and lusty, able for to fight;

* "fere" = "companion" (O.E.D.).

Now are they weak, and wearishe God he knows,
Unable now to daunt the foul despite
Which is presented by my cruel foes.
Thy thighs are thin, my body lank and lean;
It hath no bombast now, but skin and bones:
And on mine elbow as I lie and lean,
I see a trusty token for the nonce.
I spy a bracelet bound about mine arm,
Which to my shadow seemeth thus to say:
Believe not me; for I was but a charm
To make thee sleep when others went to play.
And as I gaze thus galded all with grief,
I find it fazëd* almost quite in sunder.
Then think I thus: thus wasteth my relief,
And though I fade, yet to the world, no wonder.
For as this lace by leisure learns to wear,
So must I faint, even as the candle wasteth.
These thoughts, dear sweet, within my breast I bear;
And to my long home, thus my life it hasteth.
Herewith I feel the drops of sweltering sweat
Which trickle down my face, enforced so,
And in my body feel I likewise beat
A burning heart which tosseth to and fro.
Thus all in flames I cinder-like consume,
And were it not that wanhope lends me wind,
Soon might I fret my fancies all in fume,
And like a ghost my ghost his grave might find.
But freezing hope doth blow full in my face,

* "faze" = "feaze, to unravel" also "faze, to discompose" (O.E.D.).

And cold of cares becomes my cordial,
So that I still endure that irksome place
Where sorrow seethes to scald my skin withal.

One pictures the lovelorn Englishman, with his knobby knees and knotty chest, in an oaken Tudor bathtub, sweating and weeping in a draught. This magnificent blend of comedy and self-pity suggests that the physical circumstances of life, as our senses perceive them, play certain constant roles in the poetry of all periods, however much kinds of rhetoric or kinds of image may vary historically. The body; the token of lace; the hot water and cold air, which so utterly transform the cliches of the lover who bathes in bale or feels gusts of hope; the pounding heart; the sweat—these convey some of the same feelings as the groceries, driveways, and brilliant canned goods of Ginsberg. That is, the physical world reminds us of our solitude; of mortality, which all physical things undergo but only we can meditate; of the contingency and randomness of the world the senses know; and of the truth that, as Stevens has said, the greatest poverty is not to live in a physical world.

In both poems, the counterpoint to the physical world is the lonely, comic, and tragic phenomenon of speech—even, in these instances, of speech-making. Without retracting what has been said in the foregoing pages about the special role of sensory details as they relate to statement in modern poetry, one can observe that word and thing also have a companionable, dynamic relationship that is part of the nature of things.

That relationship, of solitude and sharing, informs many of the most appealing contemporary poems. I will choose two from many. Both of them attain a proselike openness of statement while incorporating and using a distinctly contemporary sense of the material world, its obdurate inhumanity and its human uses. First, David Ferry's "The Soldier":

Saturday afternoon. The barracks is almost empty.
The soldiers are almost all on overnight pass.
There is only me, writing this letter to you,
And one other soldier, down at the end of the room,
And a spider, that hangs by the thread of his guts,
His tenacious and delicate guts, Swift's spider,
All self-regard, or else all privacy.
The dust drifts in the sunlight around him, as currents
Lie in lazy drifting schools in the vast sea.
In his little sea the spider lowers himself
Out of his depth. He is his own diving bell,
Though he cannot see well. He observes no fish,
And sees no wonderful things. His unseeing guts
Are his only hold on the world outside himself.
I love you, and miss you, and I find you hard to imagine.
Down at the end of the room, the other soldier
Is getting ready, I guess, to go out on pass.
He is shining his boots. He sits on the edge of his bunk,
Private, submissive, and heedful of himself,
And, bending over himself, he is his own nest.
The slightest sound he makes is of his being.
He is his mother, and nest, wife, brother, and father.
His boots are bright already, yet still he rubs
And rubs till, brighter still, they are his mirror.
And in this mirror he observes, I guess,
His own submissiveness. He is far from home.

The solipsism implied by observation also implies our hold on the world, because observation is also a mirror; a fellow-soldier mirrors oneself. To be even a little at home in the wordless world we work at, the voice must assemble it into a nest. That rubbing and placing of the mirror of observation frees us, somewhat, into the simplicities of speech: "I love you," and the rest of it. Between the spooky quiet of the material world and the quiet of solipsism, the poet arranges a kind of partnership, so that prose virtues—the repetitions of the word "soldier," the freedom to "guess" toward a nest made of language, observation, and memory—can conspire toward the achievement of statement. Statement is human, is a relation to others: wife, brother, and so forth.

Ferry's poem plays observation against an extreme quiet and simplicity of statement: a contemporary version of the lonely-shepherd poem. John Ashbery's "Some Trees" also plays observation against a lucid, declarative simplicity, in something like a contemporary pastoral love poem:

> These are amazing: each
> Joining a neighbor, as though speech
> Were a still performance.
> Arranging by chance
>
> To meet as far this morning
> From the world as agreeing
> With it, you and I
> Are suddenly what the trees try
>
> To tell us we are:
> That their merely being there

Means something; that soon
We may touch, love, explain.

And glad not to have invented
Such comeliness, we are surrounded:
A silence already filled with noises,
A canvas on which emerges

A chorus of smiles, a winter morning.
Placed in a puzzling light, and moving,
Our days put on such reticence
These accents seem their own defence.

The trees—merely some trees—join in a way like a vision of
effortless speech, and the poem is about joining, agreement,
sufficiency. All of these transpire only briefly: another day, re-
moval from the world and agreement with it might not happen
to coincide so clearly. In another mood, an invented comeliness
might seem preferable, or the fact that natural comeliness is no
human invention might seem less agreeable. Reticence, the ease
of simplicity and quietness, seems on this particular morning
to be both attainable and sufficient. That sufficiency of reti-
cence, and the Wordsworthian harmony between mood and
circumstance, are momentary pieces of good luck for the lov-
ers; nor do they forget that the comeliness is not their inven-
tion, and that the trees' merely being there means only this
pastoral "thing," no more. It is the "silent," or utterly reticent
noise made by the landscape of "The Snow Man," seen by pas-
toral lovers.

These poems interest me because they are traditional in a
broader, older sense than the modernist or Romantic traditions

that have been my subject. They are traditional in that broader way, successfully, partly because they have mastered their more local, immediate traditions. That is, the matter of discursive statement and "termless" detail is handled in the proportioned, natural way that comes from great conscious art. Perhaps that is simply another way of saying that I admire these poems. And yet, "shopping for images," "arranging by chance," "seeing a trusty token for the nonce," observing "I guess" another person's actions—they do seem to share a certain approach to the random swirl of external life, as it meets the demands of the spirit.

To end this ending by quoting any one particular contemporary poem seems an error of emphasis. To slither out of that problem, here is a translation, by the contemporary poet Charles Gullans, of Hugo von Hofmannsthal's "Ballade of Exterior Life," a poem of graceful, sentimental gloom about the randomness of life, with its catalogue of things and thing-like emotions. That gloriously soupy melancholy is healed, or at least resolved, by an appeal to the act of uttering a word, so that this beautifully written translation may serve as an appropriate, diminuendo close in a minor key:

Ballade of Exterior Life

And children will grow up with their deep eyes,
Who nothing know, will grow, with death their lot,
And every man will go his separate way.

And sweet fruits from the sour will be begot,
And fall like dead birds to the ground by night,
And lie their several days, until they rot.

The wind forever blows, and we incite
Our own desires, our lassitude of sense,
Forever learn new words that we recite.

And streets run through the grass, and places dense
With torchlight, trees, and ponds are here assembled
And withered with a fatal violence.

For what have these been reared? that none resemble
Another? And so many are the same?
What does it change to laugh, to weep, to tremble?

And what does all this profit us, this game,
Though we are many, we are lonely still,
And wander, searching without any aim?

To have seen so much of this will profit whom?
Yet he says much, who only says, "the evening,"
A word from which sadness and sorrow spill

Like heavy honey from the hollow combs.

NOTES

I. Introduction

1. See in particular sections III and IV of chapter III below.

2. "The Blue Booby" and "Trader" are reprinted in *The Norton Anthology of Modern Poetry*, ed. Richard Ellmann and Robert O'Clair. Hereafter, I will annotate poems only if they seem unusually difficult to locate on the basis of the poet's name, or if the poet's name does not appear in the text.

3. One persuasive, compact version of what modern poetry is might be based upon: Donald Davie's *Ezra Pound: Poet as Sculptor* (New York: Oxford, 1964), especially the chapter on "The Rock-Drill Cantos"; Graham Hough's essay "Imagism and Its Consequences," in *Image and Experience: Reflections on a Literary Revolution* (London: Duckworth, 1960); Hugh Kenner's essay "The Experience of the Eye: Marianne Moore's Tradition," *Southern Review*, October 1965; Frank Kermode's *Romantic Image* (London, Routledge, 1957); and Robert Langbaum's essay "The New Nature Poetry" in *The Modern Spirit* (New York: Oxford, 1970).

T. S. Eliot's "From Poe to Valéry" is perhaps the best introduction of all to the ideas about modernism in poetry that I have in mind.

The viewpoint suggested by my brief, somewhat arbitrary list could be described (I hope) as conservative and generous. More conservative, and less generous, is the work of Yvor Winters, whose great collection of critical essays, *In Defense of Reason* (Chicago: Swallow, 1950) does not so much complete the list as counterbalance or transform it.

My debt to the writing on this list should be clear.

4. Pound, of course, is using "abstractions" rhetorically, not philosophically. That is, he is advising poets to stay close to the senses, and he uses the term "abstractions" in the sense of "words with abstract referents" as distinct from words with concrete referents. I do not mean to imply that Pound was unaware of the quite basic point, about the nature of language, which I rehash in this paragraph.

5. Kenner, "The Experience of the Eye," 767. This essay, in a different form, is available as part of Kenner's A *Homemade World* (New York: Knopf, 1975), 91–118.

6. Robert Bly, "Silence."

7. May Swenson, "Cardinal Ideograms." The slight change in style of the poem-about-nothing, with its tedious "imaginative" quality, may be illustrated by comparing Swenson's poem with Charles Simic's more recent "Bestiary for the Fingers of My Right Hand":

> The middle one has backache.
> Stiff, still unaccustomed to this life;
> An old man at birth. It's about something
> That he had and lost,
> That he looks for within my hand,
> The way a dog looks
> For fleas
> With a sharp tooth.

8. This untitled poem or section may be found in Creeley's *Pieces*.

Chapter II

1. Paul Zweig, "The New Surrealism," in *Contemporary Poetry in America*, ed. Robert Boyers (New York: Schocken, 1947), 325.

2. Another poem of the same period, Henley's "Ballade of Dead Actors," represents a kind of far point within this tradition: virtually the only specified emotions in the overwhelmingly elegiac poem are those created by dramatists and feigned by actors now dead, with a further melancholy, nostalgic remove embodied in the poem's manner, which is deliberately archaic.

3. Two good answers to this question, pro and con, are the essay "John Berryman: An Introduction" by Martin Dodsworth in his collection *The Survival of Poetry* (London: Faber, 1970) and William Pritchard's review "Shags and Poets" (*Hudson Review*, vol. xxiii, no. 3, 563).

4. Samuel Hynes, *The Pattern of Hardy's Poetry* (Chapel Hill: University of North Carolina Press, 1961).

5. Dodsworth (*Survival of Poetry*, 116) writes: "In ... the major sense, Berryman writes far and away from, indeed in reaction to, the modernist tradition of Pound and Eliot."

6. However, Hardy's "An Ancient to Ancients" is mentioned in Dream Song 151; and in the book *Master Poems of the English Language*, ed. Oscar Williams (New York: Washington Square, 1966) Berryman chooses Hardy's "The Darkling Thrush" for his "master poem." Ransom edited and wrote an introduction for *The Selected Poems of Thomas Hardy* (New York: Macmillan, 1961).

Chapter III

1. For the background of criticism and scholarship to which these pages are particularly indebted, see note 3, chapter I.

2. It may be necessary to say something about how "free verse" pertains to the conflict between realist and nominalist attitudes toward abstract concepts. That is, it is clear that even a fairly specific group of words like "the pale green cup shattered" consists of a chain of static abstractions, since one cannot point out or experience "pale" or "cup," only particular palenesses or cups; and while the particular cup may change, "cup" just sits there. Similarly, the forms of syntax are clearly abstract. But rhythm, it may seem, can be particular, a nominalistic absolute.

However, the most basic of abstract concepts are similarity and recurrence. All forms—the repeating curve of the circle or the most subtle, free-seeming rhythm—are based on similarity, exact or slight, between particular moments.

The turning of verse to a new line means that the line-ending, presumably, has significance, even if the significance changes or is sometimes voided; and it recurs. Lines recur.

At this point, it is interesting to quote the wistful remarks of W. S. Merwin, "On Open Form":

> . . . it seems as though what is needed for any particular nebulous hope that may become a poem is not a manipulable, more or less predictably recurring pattern, but *an unduplicable resonance, something that would be like an echo except that it is repeating no sound.*
>
> (*Naked Poetry*, ed. Stephen Berg and Robert Mezey
> [New York: Bobbs-Merrill, 1969], 271, emphasis added.)

The purely particular form is a paradox or chimera.

Incidentally, the strange relation of poetry to strict measure or "number" is suggested by the title and existence, this late in the history of modernism, of the anthology from which I have quoted Merwin. The absence of rhyme and meter guides the selections (though not consistently); the title indicates that poetry not clothed in rhyme and meter seems "naked" to the editors: a good illustration of the way conventions show their force most when they are avoided.

3. Harold Bloom, *A Map of Misreading* (New York: Oxford, 1975), 3.

4. Archibald MacLeish, "Ars Poetica."

5. I cannot resist quoting the annotation of "Ars Poetica" from one such textbook, Paul Engle and Warren Carrier's *Reading Modern Poetry* (Glenview: Scott, Foresman, 1968), 75:

> ... the technique of expressing significance in poetry demands sharp, specific *detail*. The concrete symbols, the things of this world as we know it—these are the invariable stuff of poetry as, to the same extent, they need be of no other form of verbal communication. Poetry must operate through such verbal symbols [original emphasis].

It is in ways like this, and in ways even more fugitive, that traditions and the received ideas that parody those traditions enter the air we breathe.

6. Fulke Greville, "Elegy on the Death of Sidney."

7. Bernard Bergonzi, "Nature, Mostly American," *Southern Review*, Winter 1970, 205–15; and Robert Langbaum, "The New Nature Poetry," *The Modern Spirit* (New York: Oxford, 1970), 101–26.

8. The phrase "pre-Keats" of course is figurative in the sense that Keats represents an instance, not a unique discoverer of these concerns. For example, David Ferry in *The Limits of Mortality* (Middletown: Wesleyan University Press, 1959) shows how more or less the same concerns and dilemmas are dealt with by Wordsworth.

9. Robert Bly, "Driving toward the Lac Qui Parle River."

10. Tom Schmidt, "Black and White," in *New American and Canadian Poetry*, ed. John Gill (Boston: Beacon, 1971), 237.

11. But not by Ginsberg himself, who is clearly another story. Tentatively, one might say that if the poets under discussion here are at times negatively "traditional" toward Stevens, then Ginsberg stands in a similar relationship to T. S. Eliot (incantation, quasi-religious or religious attitudes, a concern for the communal spiritual health, a sense that the inherited cultural goods may be stale or spoiled).

12. *The Paris Review*, 53 (1972), 162.

13. For instance, Berton Roueché's "Profiles (The Banana)," *New Yorker*, October 1973, mentions "a medieval legend that the banana, not the apple, was the fruit

with which Eve tempted Adam." Thus, bananas are an example of a revised Biblical myth, of temptations, of subjects for *New Yorker* "Profiles."

14. See note 2 to this chapter, above.

Chapter IV

1. *Memorial Day* was published by Viking, *American Handbook* by the University of Pittsburgh Press, and *Hard Freight* by Wesleyan University Press.

2. Lawrence Raab, "The Night of the Statues," *Poetry,* vol. cxxv, no. 1, October 1974, 28.

3. This text of "Badger" is from *The Poems of John Clare,* ed. J. W. Tibble, 2 vols. (London: Dent, 1935) and is the version usually reprinted. However, there are good reasons to prefer the longer text published in *Clare: Selected Poems and Prose,* ed. Eric Robinson and Geoffrey Summerfield (London: Oxford, 1966).

The complicated editorial arguments are irrelevant here, but it is interesting to note that the Robinson and Summerfield version frames the account of the individual badger between additional first and last stanzas that are generic. The longer version loses some of the force and unity of the shorter, but extends the theme of derangement to a further extreme of pathos. Here is the additional last stanza:

Some keep a baited badger tame as hog
And tame him till he follows like the dog
They urge him on like dogs and show fair play
He beats and scarcely wounded goes away
Lapt up as if asleep he scorns to fly
And siezes any dog that ventures nigh
Clapt like a dog he never bites the men
But worrys dogs and hurrys to his den
They let him out and turn a harrow down
And there he fights the host of all the town
He licks the patting hand and trys to play
And never trys to bite or run away
And runs away from noise in hollow trees
Burnt by the boys to get a swarm of bees

Here the animal's very nature is deranged. Its combative energy or instinct to "beat" becomes a crazy reflex, ranged against the pathetic "trys to play."

4. John and Anne Tibble, *John Clare: His Life and Poetry* (London: Heinemann, 1956), 77.

5. Middleton Murry quoted in *The Poems of John Clare*, ix.

CHAPTER V

1. Richard Kostelanetz, "Conversation with Berryman," *Massachusetts Review*, XI, Spring 1970, 341.

2. Paul Zweig, "The New Surrealism," *Contemporary American Poetry*, ed. Robert Boyers (New York: Schocken, 1974), 325.

3. William Matthews, *Sleek for the Long Flight* (New York: Random House, 1972).

CREDITS

Lines of poetry by the following poets are taken from the indicated volumes:

By A. R. Ammons, from COLLECTED POEMS: 1951–1971, copyright © 1972
   A. R. Ammons, published by W. W. Norton & Co., Inc., New York, 1972.
   "Motion" and "Plunder" reprinted by permission of W. W. Norton & Co., Inc.

By John Ashbery, from SOME TREES, copyright © 1956 John Ashbery, published
   by Yale University Press, New Haven, 1956, reissued by Corinth Books, New
   York, 1970, and from THE DOUBLE DREAM OF SPRING, copyright © 1970
   John Ashbery, published by E. P. Dutton, New York, 1970. "Some Trees"
   reprinted by permission of John Ashbery.

By John Berryman, from THE DREAM SONGS, copyright © 1969 John
   Berryman, published by Farrar, Straus & Giroux, New York, 1969. "Dream
   Song 14," "Dream Song 29," "Dream Song 56" and "Dream Song 145" reprinted
   by permission of Farrar, Straus & Giroux, Inc.

By Frank Bidart, from GOLDEN STATE, copyright © 1973 Frank Bidart,
   published by George Braziller, New York, 1973.

By Elizabeth Bishop, from THE COMPLETE POEMS, copyright © 1969
   Elizabeth Bishop, published by Farrar, Straus & Giroux, New York, 1969.

By Robert Bly, from SILENCE IN THE SNOWY FIELDS, copyright © 1962
   Robert Bly, published by Wesleyan University Press, Middletown, 1962.

By Louise Bogan, from COLLECTED POEMS, copyright © 1959 Louise Bogan,
   published by Farrar, Straus & Giroux, New York, 1959. "Simple Autumnal"
   reprinted by permission of Farrar, Straus & Giroux, Inc.

By Robert Creeley, from PIECES, copyright © 1969 Robert Creeley, published by
   Charles Scribner's Sons, New York, 1969. "Could Write of Fucking" reprinted
   by permission of Charles Scribner's Sons, Inc.

By J. V. Cunningham, from THE EXCLUSIONS OF A RHYME, copyright © J. V.

Democracy, Culture and the Voice of Poetry

(2002)

To my colleagues and helpers at
The Favorite Poem Project
Boston University
236 Bay State Road

ACKNOWLEDGMENTS

I thank the Princeton University Center for Human Values for inviting me to give the Tanner Lectures, and also for providing four vital, insightful and generous public respondents. I am grateful to A. S. Byatt, Jonathan Galassi, John Hollander and Marianna De Marco Torgovnick for their engaged and imaginative discussions of what I said. This published version of the lectures has benefited from their collegiality.

This book approaches its subject partly through the Favorite Poem Project, which has depended upon the vision and support provided by Boston University, the Carnegie Education Foundation, and The National Endowment for the Arts. I am personally grateful to Cliff Becker and William Ivey at the NEA, to Vartan Gregorian at the Carnegie Foundation, and to Jon Westling, president of Boston University, who in addition to his support participated in the Project by reading and memorably discussing Wallace Stevens's poem "The Idea of Order at Key West."

Executive Producer Juanita Anderson, of Legacy Productions, surpassed expectation in producing the video segments. Jeffrey Brown, Jim Lehrer and Les Crystal of "The NewsHour with Jim Lehrer" have helped the segments find their audience.

I am indebted for their help to Christine Bauch, Emily Brandt, Rosemarie Ellis, Maggie Dietz and James Jayo.

I. Culture

The term "culture" with its old agricultural and biological connotations has taken on a new, surprising centrality. In world affairs and in American electoral politics, in geopolitical analysis and in economics, culture has become a kind of ulterior cause of causes. It has been proposed that culture determines the power of a nation to achieve economic development, and that cultural more than political differences underlie electoral contests and atrocities, economic trends and terrorist acts. Cultural clashes seem to have replaced ideological strife. Even the directions and conceptions of science have been seen in cultural terms.

Far from resisting this trend, I want to consider the voice of poetry—emphasizing its literal or actual "voice"—within the culture of American democracy, amid the tensions of pluralism.

The art of poetry has many of its roots in hierarchical, predemocratic culture: the flirtations and imperial visions of European courts; the monkish preservations of scholars, the wistful, stylized perception of Asian officials and monks, the folk-narratives, charms and ballads of peasants. Poetry's place in the United States—often presented, I think inaccurately, as no place—presents a node of anxieties about culture itself and about the idea of democracy.

In its long-ago, rather frumpy state, the term "culture"—as in the antiquated phrase "a person of culture"—generated no aura of dread (despite Marxist or Freudian analysis of the mere social fear that one might seem "uncultured"). In its contemporary form, however, the notion of culture evokes anxiety of two contradictory, more or less opposite, kinds.

On one side, there is the nightmare of undifferentiation, a loss of cultural diversity comparable to the loss of biodiversity. Hundreds of languages have died in the last century, with their alphabets and epics and delicate structures. In the terrible closing pages of *Tristes Tropiques*, Claude Levi-Strauss indicates how the mere breath, the very glance, of the observer rapidly destroys differences that evolved for centuries, homogenizing and sterilizing the former abundance. This vision of destruction by an all-consuming dominant culture reminds us of the etymological link between "culture" and the "*colon*": the one who cultivates or scratches the soil, the colonialist.

Closer to home, in the market-generated mass culture that is a successful export, we can see something that resembles the irresistible domination of the colonizers who sweep away and drown out and plow under the ancient range of cultural variety: a kind of internal colonialism, the image of a dominating uniformity that threatens to macerate distinction and level terrain until all are the same.

But the other, obverse dread is of a vicious, tribalized factionalism, the coming apart of civic fabrics through fragmentation, ranging from the tremendous, paranoid brutalities of ethnic cleansing and ruthless terrorism to the petty division of mass culture into niches. Religious difference, racial difference, linguistic difference, even generational difference can seem compounded and hypertrophied by information-age forces. The fanatical concentration on difference and its exploitation by tyranny have been multiplied, accelerated and terribly empowered by modern technology. For example, the speed and reach of contemporary broadcast propaganda have sometimes fit neatly with the activities of killing squads. In this disturbing area, the etymological ghost is culture's relation to "cult," a word denoting arcane forms of worship: the perceived sinister difference of strangers, its ultimate evolution a zeal for extermination.

And here, too, there is a kind of inward, domestic corollary, a dread that goes beyond the breakdown of bowling leagues and civic clubs. In the local microcosm, the cult of xenophobia has its parallels in the paranoid dread of new democratic generations as subliterate media savages. The fear of our own young as letterless, unassimilable barbarians is perhaps an extreme vernacular form of this emotion.

Such are the opposed nightmares of *colon* and cult: fear of suffocation by a centralized overknitting on one side and fear of murderous unraveling from the fringes on the other. These fears—and who can be immune to them?—reflect a profound ambivalence about culture itself, which like the goddess Kali-Parvati both nurtures and destroys. The concept of culture, Stephen Greenblatt has pointed out, "gestures toward what appear to be opposite things: *constraint* and *mobility*"*—normative terms roughly parallel to the uniformities of the colonialist

---

* *Critical Terms for Literary Study*, ed. Frank Lentricchia and Thomas McLaughlin (Chicago: University of Chicago Press, 1995).

and the fanatacisms of the cultist. We are simultaneously afraid of constraints making us so much like one another that we will lose something vital in our human nature, and also in fear of becoming so fluently different, so much divided into alien and brutally competitive fragments, gangs or fabricated nationalisms, that we cannot survive. In what ways do these opposed, even contradictory cultural anxieties share a single source?

For an American poet, the fear of lost differentiation and the fear of excessive differentiation do indeed embody a single, in fact familiar, anxiety: that of being cut off from memory—forgotten. The shimmering presences of American mass culture, pervasive and ephemeral, make a peculiar context for an art associated with memory—with mnemonic rhymes, with the mother of the Muses, perhaps with epics and sagas. American memory is so jagged, so polyglot—often so phantasmagorical—that it has sometimes been thought not to exist. A complementary supposition is that American poetry is cut off from American cultural reality.

Unlike memory in a pre-democratic national saga or myth, memory in our high and low cultures contains an element of self-negation, a release not into meanings or destinies but into fantasy. Gabriel García Márquez has said that the best novel written about Latin America is *The Hamlet*, by William Faulkner. That statement is not only a tribute to the seeds of magic realism in that great novel, but to the quicksilver, recklessly fabulous nature of Faulkner's historical imagination. Faulkner's South—or the South of D. W. Griffith or of Toni Morrison—like the West of cowboy movies, the suburbia of classic sitcoms, all have a dreamlike or delirious quality that is conventionally misnamed "mythic."

When Hart Crane concludes his "Proem: To Brooklyn Bridge" with the line "And of the curveship lend a myth to God," he is explicitly writing not a myth but a fantastic invocation of myth itself, a beseeched transformation of "God" and "bridge" and "us lowliest." And the city of Crane or of Ralph Ellison, as much as the city in American gangster movies or screwball comedies, is based not merely on any historical New York or Chicago or San Francisco or Los Angeles, but on the City as a dreamscape of possibilities: a brick and mortar embodiment less of the past than of desire, and more as chorus or antagonist than as a specific, fixed setting. Like the Western town of the movies always about to be tamed, endlessly at the cusp of potential, the City is a civic dream.

But it is historical memory that tempers both of the imagined extremes of culture, the barely habitable polarities of total undifferentiation and total fragmentation. Memory resists uniformity because it registers fine gradations; memory resists the factional because it registers the impure, recombining, fluent nature of culture. It is memory that eventually undermines the apparently total successes of both the colonializing Conquistador and the leveling Visigoth. The fantastic element in democratic memory exaggerates the anxieties of uniformity and fragmentation. Accustomed to practicing an ancient, singular art amid a dazzling mass culture, the American poet is a kind of veteran of these anxieties.

(A theory of American poetry itself could be based on the polarity of cult and *colon*. The fragmentation, ellipsis and implosion of referentiality that have been presented as an experimental or avant-garde style for nearly a hundred years resist the *colon*, the complacent central uniformity. The styles of an often desperate, Anglophile urbanity or an amiable middlebrow accessibility conduct an equally heroic—or at least embattled—resistance to cultural dissolution, a breakdown into provinces and cults.)

The most profound observers of the United States have seen in our manners, and in the cultural correlatives of our democracy, a version of fragmentation, the dread that we become too unlike one another. Alexis de Tocqueville, in the locus classicus for this viewpoint, associates the separation of individuals into fragments or atoms horizontally, from their peers, with the separation of individuals vertically, from their past and future. Tocqueville writes:

> Thus not only does democracy make every man forget his ancestors, but it hides his descendants and separates his contemporaries from him; it throws him back forever upon himself alone and threatens in the end to confine him entirely within the solitude of his own heart.*

This passage recalls the great classical tag, found in *Gulliver's Travels* as well as in *King Lear*, which notes that the human animal is a puny creature: its patchy fur and flimsy hide give inadequate protection; its claws and little teeth are poor weapons. It is a mediocre climber and swimmer, and even its best specimens cannot run as fast as the young or aged of many other species.

This commonplace trope—stripping the human animal of its cultural armature—is traditionally deployed to emphasize certain redeeming human qualities, such as the capacity for reason, free will, or civilization. It is also deployed, as by Lear on the heath, to demonstrate ultimate human frailty and depen-

---

* *Democracy in America*, ed. Phillips Bradley (New York: Knopf, 1945), p. 99.

dence. Tocqueville, in comparing democracy with aristocratic culture, paints the isolation of the single heart in a wilderness that is temporal as well as spatial. To be thrown back "forever" on oneself alone suggests a degree of mobility, a freedom from constraint and dependence, that is potentially exhilarating as well as deranging: a liberation, as well as a void.

That void in its terrible, bleak aspect seems to be in keeping with Tocqueville's most explicit pronouncement about American poetry—a pronouncement that, out of context, as it is usually quoted, can seem comically harsh:

> Nothing conceivable is so petty, so insipid, so crowded with paltry interests—in one word, so anti-poetic—as the life of a man in the United States. (*Democracy in America*, p. 74)

But in fact Tocqueville, after observing that the principle of equality "has dried up most of the old springs of poetry," proceeds to ask "what new ones it may disclose." Legends of heroes and gods or angels and demons, old traditions and rituals, all viable material for the poet in aristocratic societies, he says, will not serve poetry in America. He has an interesting notion about the first thing poets in the new world would turn to:

> When skepticism had depopulated heaven, and the progress of equality had reduced each individual to smaller and better-known proportions, the poets, not yet aware of what they could substitute for the great themes that were departing together with the aristocracy, turned their eyes to inanimate nature. As they lost sight of gods and heroes, they set themselves to describe streams and mountains. . . . Some have thought that this embellished delineation of all the physical and inanimate objects which cover the

earth was the kind of poetry peculiar to democratic ages. But I believe this to be an error, and that it belongs only to a period of transition.

I am persuaded that in the end democracy diverts the imagination from all that is external to man and fixes it on man alone. Democratic nations may amuse themselves for a while with considering the productions of nature, but they are excited in reality only by a survey of themselves. Here, and here alone, the true sources of poetry among such nations are to be found. . . . Among a democratic people poetry will not be fed with legends or the memorials of old traditions. . . . All these resources fail him; but Man remains, and the poet needs no more. The destinies of mankind, man himself taken aloof from his country and his age and standing in the presence of Nature and of God, with his passions, his doubts, his rare prosperities and inconceivable wretchednesses, will become the chief, if not the sole, theme of poetry among these nations. (*Democracy in America*, pp. 75–76)

And in a rather ringing final paragraph to his chapter, Tocqueville concludes:

Such are the poems of democracy. The principle of equality does not, then, destroy all the subjects of poetry: it renders them less numerous, but more vast.

This is a startling declaration by its aristocratic author. Even if one has no interest whatsoever in the art of poetry, the movement of the passage's argument should be arresting. Tocqueville's progress from "petty . . . insipid . . . anti-poetic" to "the destinies of mankind" and materials "less numerous, but more

vast" traces an ambitiously prophetic (if perhaps morally am-
biguous) trajectory for American culture—pluralistic, omnivo-
rous, syncretic.

I interpret this passage as suggesting not exactly the absence
of legends, memorials, heroes, and pantheons but their insuf-
ficiency: a worn, jejune quality—a need for something either
more candid, or more candidly fantastic. The "old memorials"
do not feed the democratic imagination, with its skepticism and
isolation. In practice, the inadequacy of "the great themes that
were departing together with the aristocracy" has inspired vari-
ous myth-making projects, including Longfellow's honorable
but doomed attempt to make indigenous versions of the "great
themes" by way of Paul Revere or Hiawatha. A more enduring
invention has been Walt Whitman's extravagant and unrealized
idea of the democratic bard—hardly "aloof from his country"
but as surely concentrated on the independent human figure,
alone with God and Nature, as—equally unmythical, equally
rooted in longing—the secularized devotional quatrains of
Emily Dickinson.

What Tocqueville's paragraphs say about subject matter in
democracy is not merely prophetic of the formal and moral ec-
centricities of Whitman and Dickinson: her skewed hymns, his
breakaway arias. Beyond poetry itself, Tocqueville's idea of
democratic nations turning toward a "survey of themselves"
raises large questions of constraint and mobility, order and lib-
erty, selfishness and community. Poetry and our ideas about it
may offer ways to inspect characteristic dramas of our national
life. This Tocqueville passage about poetry and the individual
soul adds an historical aspect to certain qualities of poetry that
contrast with, perhaps even resist, a mass-scale cultural leveling.

Though poetry's history may link it to hierarchical, pre-democratic societies, the bodily nature of poetry links it to the democratic idea of individual dignity. That dual nature of the art gives it a unique significance in the cultural dramas of particularism and universalism, individual and mass.

I don't mean to put popular culture on one side and poetry on another. The drama between human scale and mass scale is embedded to some degree in every modern work. An entire genre of dystopic science-fiction cinema is based on this polarity. The hypnotic mania and unfathomable persistences of minstrel show and sitcom, country music, vaudeville and be-bop reflect that drama, as do similar qualities in our poetry, in the work of poets as different as T. S. Eliot and Allen Ginsberg. The art the poets practice has a special poignance in a society that emphasizes the idea of the individual in the very act of dreaming on an unprecedented mass scale—and so too in a different way do the plaintive, introspective works in "popular idioms" by such artists as Buster Keaton and Charlie Parker. Poetry reflects, perhaps concentrates, the American idea of individualism as it encounters the American experience of the mass—because the art of poetry by its nature operates on a level as profoundly individual as a human voice.

Lyric poetry has been defined by the unity and concentration of a solitary voice—such as might be accompanied by the sound of a lyre, a harp small enough to be held in one hand. It is singular, if not solitary. But the vocality of poetry, involving the mind's energy as it moves toward speech, and toward incantation, also involves the creation of something like—indeed, precisely *like*—a social presence. The solitude of lyric, almost by the nature of human solitude and the human voice, invokes a social presence.

Delivered as a Tanner Lecture on Human Values at Princeton University, April 5–6, 2001. Printed with permission of the Tanner Lectures on Human Values, a Corporation, University of Utah, Salt Lake City, Utah.

II. Vocality

Dire abandonment, I have read, often makes institutionalized souls, especially children, croon and rock rhythmically: a heartbroken ritual music, a making, a fearsomely minimal created presence. A clinical name for this behavior is auto-stimulation. The embarrassing hint of masturbation in that term, the grotesque unease or nervous giggle of the association, perhaps reveals an eerie recognition. Just outside the membrane enclosing that wounded isolation, made vivid by contrast, is my ordinary consciousness: engaged yet furtive, communicative yet shamed, teeming with a host of wants and taboos—the word "taboo" embodying the price of our charmed admission to the world of ordinary social stimuli. The regular cadence of the outcast creates a rudimentary other, an illusion of response, that we recognize; the covert sexual fantasies of what we call normal life exemplify a similar principle, the imagination's work of mimesis. The normal soul, too, populates itself with cadences.

The regular, monotonous chant of the abandoned recalls certain vocalizations of our humdrum solitude: say, little repetitious charms of invocation amid the nuisance of some misplaced object—*keys keys keys keys keys*; or the staccato repetition of a one-syllable obscenity, like a muttered ceremony of rage or desperation; or the happier spells of unthwarted celebration, recited at good news or some gratifying experience (*yes yes yes yes yes*); or—perhaps most interesting of all, and closest to the cadenced moans of the devastated—the little half-sung noises we may chant to ease a painful awareness, the pang of embarrassment. My memory of a truly grade-A faux pas can make me half-whisper a syllable like "*dah*" in *prestissimo* monotone to the rhythm of *The Stars and Stripes Forever* or *The Mexican Hat Dance.*

These ephemeral protopoems share a rich duality with the auto-stimulation of total distress. The unvarying, solitary rocking or crooning, with its reduction or stylization, perhaps substitutes mimetically for its opposite: a varying, attentive social presence, listening as I lament my lost car keys, curse my mistake, or celebrate the letter announcing good news. The rhythm is like an other, attending to me.

In embarrassment, the tuneless tune I murmur brings back the social world where I brought shame on myself, and imitates the all-too-responsive real presence of others—but in a rudimentary, dwindling simulacrum that distracts me from the awfulness of the actual remembered scene: a tiny cultural creation, attempting to displace or transform memory. And this little mimesis, like the cadenced grunts of loss, has its parallel in poetry.

Nervous muttering resembles a work of art in that it simultaneously sharpens and dislocates a feeling, calling it up but transforming it, maybe blunting it a little by incorporation and mimesis. Insofar as rhythm and repetition accomplish this double action, the little repeated, one-word protopoem differs significantly from anecdote. Anecdote is sociable; perhaps narrative itself is sociable. Life among others in a novel, even a novel entirely in dialogue, is in some essential way *told-about*. The novel overtly tells us what people say and do, immersing us in social reality with an illusion of presentation. In a play, presentation is actual: communal reality, in theatrical performance, exists both as though it were happening and as actually happening.

In a poem, the social realm is invoked with a special intimacy at the barely voluntary level of voice itself. Communal life, whether explicitly included or not, is present implicitly in the cadences and syntax of language: a somatic ghost. In such a theory, the Industrial-Revolution art form, fiction, reflects the conversation or letters of middle-class people in a town or city: the panicked verbosity of Pamela, the homey enumerations of Robinson Crusoe, the word-wound, shopper-like roaming of Leopold Bloom, all create a social scene from the manufactured web of discourse. The older form of theater is more like a ritual: performance creating actual presences. Maybe that is why theater so often involves the cloying yet somehow apt word "magic." The social world in poetry, according to this paradigm, is neither told about nor presented: it is, precisely, *invoked*: brought into being by the voice. Incantation, rather than the presentation of telling or ritual.

Of course, real works tend to blur or even explode such formulations, defying tidy generic modes of social reality. So too do new forms: film art and opera, both of them influencing and influenced by literature, can give presence a virtually assaultive vividness, as enveloping and fluid as dreams. Technologies like film and broadcast media dismantle any tidy definition of art forms from without, as artists do from within. We routinely recognize qualities in a novel as "poetic" or in a poem as "novelistic" or "dramatic."

Nevertheless, the kinds of art retain attributes, with characteristic terrains—and something deep in poetry operates at the borderland of body and mind, sound and word: double-region of the subtle knot that Donne says makes us man. George Oppen calls up that transitional territory in the fifth section of his poem "Of Being Numerous," with bold contrasts and overlaps among physical fact, cultural artifact, and mind itself:

> The great stone
> Above the river
> In the pylon of the bridge
>
> '1875'
>
> Frozen in the moonlight
> In the frozen air over the footpath, consciousness
>
> Which has nothing to gain, which awaits nothing,
> Which loves itself.

This passage gains in physicality from the abstract—or at least formal—chiasmic arrangement of vowel-sounds and words in the phrases "frozen in the moonlight / in the frozen air" and "nothing to gain, which awaits nothing." Pronouncing such symmetries audibly, or feeling their virtual sound, quickens our sense of physical breath stirring into social speech: the poetic quality that poets writing about their art have associated with a conversation heard through a door, a drunken song a few streets away, a distant singer in a foreign tongue. The chiasm of "nothing to gain . . . awaits nothing" is an artifact like the bridge, recognized before it is interpreted.

Even a dramatic monologue, or a narrated dialogue like Frost's "Home Burial," makes its voice or voices present to our imagination partly in the half-conscious way I have attributed to poetry: somatically, by invocation, by something akin to the inward reflex of auto-stimulation or the outward wince of embarrassment, a mimesis in rhythmical sound of social life. In Frost's poem, the blank verse becomes more than a vehicle; it is a physical presence: as corporeal as the infant's corpse at the center of the poem's marital argument, and as conventional as the social world that surrounds and infiltrates that same argument. The play of the social and the intuitive is part of the couple's contention, and it is manifest in their voices:

'God, what a woman! And it's come to this,
A man can't speak of his own child that's dead.'

'You can't because you don't know how to speak.
If you had any feelings, you that dug
With your own hand—how could you?—his little grave;
I saw you from that very window there,
Making the gravel leap and leap in air,
Leap up, like that, like that, and land so lightly
And roll back down the mound beside the hole.
I thought, Who is that man? I didn't know you.
And I crept down the stairs and up the stairs
To look again, and still your spade kept lifting.
Then you came in. I heard your rumbling voice
Out in the kitchen, and I don't know why,

But I went near to see with my own eyes.
You could sit there with the stains on your shoes
Of the fresh earth from your own baby's grave
And talk about your everyday concerns.
You had stood the spade up against the wall
Outside there in the entry, for I saw it.'

'I shall laugh the worst laugh I ever laughed.
I'm cursed. God, if I don't believe I'm cursed.'

This passage of fewer than two hundred words—barely room
for a prose narration to clear its throat—establishes forcefully
the two contending people with their agonized grief, and within
both of the agonists two elements contending for recognition:
physical reality on one side, and sensitive decorum or ceremony
on the other. Both elements are in the verse. The extreme com-
pression, the more remarkable because the dialogue is credible
as speech, is enabled by a physical component, by the artist's
arrangements of vocal noises at the threshold of consciousness.
The occasional end-rhyme is the least of it: "I saw you from that
very window there, / Making the gravel leap and leap in air, /
Leap up, like that, like that, and land so lightly / And roll back
down the mound beside the hole." Analysis can trace such steps
only clumsily and approximately: it is not only the syncopation
of repeated words, and not only the vowel in "down the mound"
but the contrasting vowel of "hole" that ends the sentence with
a rather thudlike rhyme on "roll."

In a way, the most powerful moment in this conversation is
a strange, apparent irrelevance, just before the closing. She has
said that "one is alone" and "dies more alone," that "Friends
make pretense of following to the grave, / But before one is in

it, their minds are turned. . . ." His speech in response culminates in the bizarre line, "Amy! There's someone coming down the road!"

After what she has just said about the underlying frailty, even hypocrisy, of human attachments—"The world's evil"—his sudden, exclamatory concern about a passing neighbor or stranger is grotesque, pathetic, absurd in a way that is quite like life. Embarrassment—a halting consciousness of other people, the sudden barricade of social awareness, obstructing emotion and threatening to take over the mind—is in a way the most basic, irreducible manifestation of social reality. For Frost's characters it is both an obtrusion on their argument and part of its essence. In this unexpected line, bursting from the character as he is about to be left, embarrassment and abandonment—social parallels to the cultural dreads of uniformity and dissolution—conjoin.

III. Self-Consciousness

To some extent, poetry always includes the social realm because poetry's very voice evokes the attentive presence of some other, or its lack: an auditor, significantly absent or present. And in twentieth-century American poetry's incorporation of explicit social material, the tension of social embarrassment and isolation—like the cultural tension of uniformity and dissolution—recurs in our endlessly varying struggles between stereotypes and freedoms, snobberies and realities: an intricate, ineffable process, endlessly banal and aspiring, dire and zany.

The Favorite Poem Project, which became a document (and an example) of that process, began as my response to the peculiar title Poet Laureate Consultant in Poetry to the Library of Congress. The first plan was to make audio recordings of visitors to Washington from around the country, with each person saying the words of a favorite poem and saying something about the poem. In a way by accident, this undertaking filled needs and exerted attractions that led to the remarkable video segments (produced by Juanita Anderson) shown on "The NewsHour with Jim Lehrer"; to the anthology *Americans'*

Favorite Poems; and also to thousands of favorite-poem readings, including one at the White House where the readers included then-President Clinton (Emerson's "Concord Hymn") and Hillary Rodham Clinton (Nemerov's "The Makers"), along with District of Columbia schoolchildren and a disabled war veteran (Frost's "Stopping By Woods on a Snowy Evening").

The project is an ongoing archive and an unsystematic (though in its own way ambitious) undertaking, and in no way a statistical survey. But in relation to embarrassment and isolation, uniformity and dissolution, it is interesting that one of the most widely admired poems named by participants, written about by readers of very different ages and levels of sophistication, is "The Love Song of J. Alfred Prufrock," a poem that probes social isolation and social terror with an indelible eloquence. Many high school students seem to intuit that the poem was written by a very young man—Eliot inventing a middleaged, first-person protagonist as vehicle for the sexual and social diffidence of youth.

Eliot's poem is of course about many other things beside sexual and social fears. For example, it is about culture itself as a burden, as oppressively controlling and crippling as it is enabling—a demanding performance, or at best a diverting performance. Prufrock, that monster of embarrassment, in this sense is very close to the figure of the exhausted aesthete, the wistful dandy. If he had confidence, he might be a dandy: the opposite or reverse of the embarrassed one. For the dandy, experience is somewhat tainted or corrupted by culture. (Though Oscar Wilde might reverse that statement.) As embarrassment is akin to abandonment—feeling excessively distinct from the attentive social world—the aesthete's jadedness is a feeling of sameness. In the terms of Wallace Stevens's "The Man Whose Pharynx Was Bad":

> Mildew of summer and the deepening snow
> Are both alike in the routine I know.

This is partly the voice of the Romantic life of sensation, after it has reached a state of exhaustion. It is an exaggerated, comic version of the premodern poets—Swinburne, Dowson?—who were the immediate predecessors of the Modernist generation. Frost parodies that hypersensitive aesthete in himself, writing in "To Earthward":

> I craved strong sweets, but those
> Seemed strong when I was young.
> The petal of the rose
> It was that stung.

The expressively inverted syntax, "The petal of the rose / it was that stung," is like a gently derisive tone of voice.

What is the point of parodying the dandy or aesthete in one-self, for Eliot or Stevens or Frost? It is, partly, a way of parodying both poetry itself and the democratic culture that offers no ready place for poetry. Like embarrassment (and like the warning "There's someone coming down the road!") the hyperbolic figure of the dandy acknowledges the presence of others and the tension aroused by that presence. I hear this serious joke on the voice of poetry in William Carlos Williams, too. In "These," a poem partly about pathos and death, he writes the terrible then momentarily comical lines:

the people gone that we loved,
the beds lying empty, the couches
damp, the chairs unused—

Hide it away somewhere
out of the mind, let it get roots
and grow, unrelated to jealous

ears and eyes—for itself.
In this mine they come to dig—all.
Is this the counterfoil to sweetest

music? The source of poetry that
seeing the clock stopped, says,
The clock has stopped

that ticked yesterday so well?

Of course all clocks, before they stop, tick—presumably "well."
The rhetorical question, repeating the observation, resembles
the ancient wisecrack about even a stopped clock being right
twice a day. The poem evokes the terror of death and loss, and
then for a moment questions elegy and all other attempts to
verbalize loss, as tautological or obvious. "Stupidity" has been
an element in the poem from the rhetorical snap of its opening
sentence:

> *These*
>
> are the desolate, dark weeks
> when nature in its barrenness
> equals the stupidity of man.

The audacity of this, like the almost-parodic repetition of "the clock has stopped," has a virtuoso quality, in its deadpan, downright way almost as dandified as Stevens's exotic ambushes of vocabulary. There is even a note of the exquisite or dandy in the rarefied word "counterfoil," which sounds like a term from music or fencing but denotes the stub of a check, where the date and amount are recorded.

Like one who recalls "The petal of the rose / It was that stung," and like the sensibility that finds the white of summer mildew and the white of snow "alike," Williams's voice here momentarily concedes an embarrassing absurdity in its discourse, and in the roots of its discourse. The stopped clock once ticked well, then it stopped—poetry sees this and in effect strikes its brow, speaking its question to marvel at the obvious. It is a moment that places poetry into something a little like a roomful of people, with Williams simultaneously among them, regarding poetry as quizzically as any, but also presenting its power to them—as he does with the two lines that follow the relatively comic question:

> The source of poetry that
> seeing the clocked has stopped, says
> The clock has stopped
>
> that ticked yesterday so well?
> and hears the sound of lakewater
> splashing—that is now stone.

With characteristic speed, restlessly varying idioms and levels, Williams takes the memorializing gesture from somewhat hapless record-keeping—the counterfoil noting the stopped clock—to a somber image, with a kind of classical dignity.

The aesthete, stung by the petal, seeing the mildew and the snow as alike, is in a way the poet reduced to a social type. In these poems, a touch of the hyperbolically exquisite allows poetry to acknowledge its own nature: by some social standards, an art of preposterous, goofball metonymies and far-fetched resemblances. In a mode that is a mirror-reversal of the dandyish, it sees the clock has stopped and says, "The clock has stopped," adding that it ticked quite well yesterday. In each case, a tiny particle of social comedy infuses a brilliant phrase. The self-consciously dandyish and its mock-naive reversal both acknowledge poetry's exorbitant, nearly embarrassing qualities and at the same time make those qualities irresistible and even—because they have a social meaning—somehow familiar.

Poetry, then, has roots in the moment when a voice makes us alert to the presence of another or others. It has affinities with all the ways a solitary voice, actual or virtual, imitates the presence of others. Yet as a form of art it is deeply embedded in the single human voice, in the solitary state that hears the other and sometimes recreates that other. Poetry is a vocal imagining, ultimately social but essentially individual and inward.

Insofar as Tocqueville was prescient about American poetry's concentration on the human soul, "aloof" from society and from ages, there is perhaps a special drama in our poetry to this play between social and individual, outward and inward voice. Elizabeth Bishop delineates that drama explicitly and compactly in the crucial passage of her poem "In the Waiting Room":

Suddenly, from inside,
came an *oh!* of pain
—Aunt Consuelo's voice—
not very loud or long.
I wasn't at all surprised;
even then I knew she was
a foolish, timid woman.
I might have been embarrassed,
but wasn't. What took me
completely by surprise
was that it was *me*:
my voice, in my mouth.
Without thinking at all
I was my foolish aunt,
I—we—were falling, falling,
our eyes glued to the cover
of the *National Geographic*,
February, 1918.

The voice comes "from inside"—inside the dentist's office and inside the child. The possible embarrassment ("I might have been ... / but wasn't") may be prevented by the strangeness of this moment, which could be a primal moment for poetry, or for individual consciousness, or both. As she begins to faint, the child gazes at the undifferentiated landscape of "shadowy gray knees, / trousers and skirts and boots / and different pairs of hands" and asks "Why should I be my aunt, / or me, or anyone? / What similarities. . . . / held us all together / or made us all just one?" The bizarre, alien assemblage of knees and boots, trousers and skirts presents a vision of the social world outside the self, fragmentary and dizzily provisional. The *National Geographic*, that homey compendium of exotic cultures, can offer nothing stranger—or more enigmatically, repellently intimate—than these familiar garments and body parts, in the cultural practices of neck-binding or cannibalism.

What makes us all one—and what makes us all different—seems deeply involved with a voice: a voice that is both imagined and actual; both inner and social; both mine and someone else's; that separates me and includes me. It will not do to sentimentalize this voice; at the climax of Bishop's poem is the sentence "The War was on." Each of these dualities involves struggle, perhaps even combat. But the voice of poetry is uniquely situated as audible yet not necessarily performative.

The voice of poetry, as in "In the Waiting Room," is intimate, on an individual scale, but far from solipsistic. It penetrates and in a sense originates where the reader's mind reaches toward something heard or uttered as though vocality were one of the senses. This medium is different from performance: different from the poet's intonations and personality shining forth at a poetry reading, and different from a skilled actor's gifts. The voice is inside a reader, but gestures outward. Though in many ways it resembles the performer's art, it is in other ways the opposite of that art, for the voice of poetry, though it may be social—and of course has been gloriously theatrical—ultimately begins as profoundly interior. The theatrical art of performance, manifestly and immediately social, moves inward from without, penetrating toward the interior from the spectacularly audible, visible presence. Poetry proceeds in the opposite direction.

IV. Performance

This intimacy and human scale of poetry have special meaning within a mass culture extraordinarily rich in performance—a society where show business and performing arts provide a major industry, a de facto aristocracy, and an all-but-universal measure of things. The mass culture of our democracy, our standard arena for expressing the anxieties of cult and *colon*, is a mighty achievement. And its works have included poetry and been included in poetry. But poetry also plays a significant role as a contrast to mass culture—somewhat resistant precisely because the poetic medium is essentially individual.

This contrast explains the frequency with which poets are asked a certain question. In its various forms, it is the question that the news media cannot easily resist asking any poet. This inevitable inquiry, however it is presented, amounts to: shouldn't poetry be part of show business? Or even, why does poetry seem out of step with the entertainment industry?

And because the query is wrongheaded, asks why poetry is not something other than itself, one's answers are feeble. The form of the question might be, "Have your poems been set to music?" Well yes, but to paraphrase a great poet, I thought I was doing that when I wrote them. Or, "What about the look of the poem on the page, as visual art?" Fine, attend to it—but as a division of graphics poetry is rather arcane and precious; as an art it is central and major. Or, "What do you think of rap music?" Don't know much about it, but my guess is that as with "literary" poetry, most of it is ordinary, a little of it is very good and a little is contemptible. I have heard Yusef Komunyakaa express distrust of it insofar as it makes a commodity out of rage. "And poetry slams?" Probably a good thing for poetry, though as part of the entertainment industry poetry will always be cute and small; as an art it is immense and fundamental.

But the interrogation is hopeless, because it begins with the assumption that poetry's tremendous strength, in the democratic context—that is, its human scale, its distinction from show business—is its weakness. Poetry as breath penetrates to where the body recognizes the stirring of meaning. Poetry mediates, on a particular and immensely valuable level, between the inner consciousness of the individual reader and the outer world of other people. To take poetry altogether away from that profound terrain to the culturally prominent, more familiar platform of performance is to tame it, because poetry is vocal, but not necessarily performative. The voice of poetry is profoundly resistant to American culture, yet uniquely inside us, as well.

V. Social Presence

I have said that poetry penetrates to where the body recognizes the stirring of meaning. The English language lacks an auditory parallel to "visualization," but in that nameless action of imagining the audible shapes of meanings a crucial human power dwells.

That power is social as well as psychological. If all art is imitation, what does the art of verse imitate? It imitates the social actions of meaning. (This mimesis is all the more distinct if the poem is difficult or aspires to the "nonreferential.") The cadences of poetry mime the shapes of our sentences, our meaningful grunts of exclamation, interrogation, direction, complaint. A line both is and imitates an utterance. (I borrow this idea from John Thompson's brilliant and seminal book *The Founding of English Meter*.) A poem simultaneously says something and in its sounds imitates the action of saying something.

This dual energy acknowledges meaning as a doubly communal phenomenon: communal in one way insofar as it embodies cultural forms, and in another way insofar as it communicates social meanings. To put it differently, in its interior way the voice of poetry is like speaking, but also like watching oneself speak, from another terrain. The stylized, mimetic component, inter-acting with the discursive component, resembles the kind of cognition athletes call "body-knowledge" or musicians refer to as "getting it under your fingers." The poem brings unconscious, inward knowing together with conscious, outward knowing.

As a practical matter, this means that to memorize a poem, or even to say it aloud, or even to "visualize" it in your imaginary voice, schools us in the shapes of meaning. In the singular temporal rhythms of verse, the shapes of meaning become body-knowledge. I wonder if anyone who has memorized a lot of poetry, or heard a lot of it, can fail to write coherent sentences and paragraphs? Possibly, the difficulty many people have in writing sentences manifests a lack of bodily exercise, breath executing patterns of meaning. We try to correct the condition with drills and abstract instructions. Why and how might a professional soldier like Ulysses S. Grant come to write so well? Could it reflect the fact that nineteenth-century Americans recited a lot of poetry, so that the mimesis of meaning came into the region we designate as in our bones or under our skin? Whether that speculation is right or wrong, the ancient relation between poetry and education, verse and understanding, deserves reconsideration.

But this curricular or pedagogical musing is only tangential to the ways poetry's double-nature, simultaneously internal and social, discourse and mimesis, is related to its place in the culture of a democracy. It is time to say something more about The Favorite Poem Project, which invited Americans to submit the title and author of a poem they admired enough to say aloud for a national audio and video archive, and to write a few sentences about the poem's personal importance or significance.

The project has been described in a well-meaning way as an attempt to "promote" or "advance" poetry in the United States, but in fact the main idea was in a sense more passive, and in my opinion more profound: to reflect some of the social presence of poetry in the lives of Americans—implicitly, in relation to our cultural anxieties.

That presence has been doubted, and beyond question the life of poetry has not always been highly visible in the United States—for complex cultural reasons I'll try to sketch. Some people used to envy, and perhaps sentimentalize, the highly visible Soviet-era poetry readings held in Russian sports stadiums and attended by audiences of many thousands. But those events depended not only upon state manipulation and financing, but upon the exploitation of ancient tastes and attitudes: specifically, the stadium readings joined the power of a bureaucratic dictatorship with the cachet of poetry in a country where an angry driver may shout at another "You have no culture!" This is not an American insult. We must strain our imaginations to conceive of countries where the politicians must at least pretend to love the great national poet, and perhaps memorize a line or two. To put it differently, the art has had little snob value among us.

Relatively speaking, in the United States the high bourgeoisie has not preened itself on curatorship of poetry. Nor do we have a single, unifying folk culture—the alternative to a social class that considers itself to have a curatorial role by heredity. The Italian-American grandmother, the Cuban-American grandmother, the Yankee grandmother, the African-American grandmother will pass on different jokes and recipes and rhymes, insofar as they are in the somewhat rare position to pass on anything. And this hypothesis of distinct ethnic or cultural categories is far more pure than our actual, fluid reality.

In place of the aristocratic idea and the folk idea, we have, characteristically, improvised and patched together a place for art and for the art of poetry, in various ways—journalistic, middle-class–domestic, professionalized, academic, self-conscious. The history of this process is reflected by John Hollander's admirable two-volume anthology of nineteenth-century American verse in the Library of America series. ("Verse" is the term Hollander preferred for the title; the publishers insisted on "Poetry," the more honorific word obscuring the social history. Indeed, this little debate is itself part of that history.) The American invention of Creative Writing as a course of study is one example of that improvisation: a means of curating the art, and extending it socially, in the absence of the social institutions and attitudes of Eastern Europe or Asia or Latin America.

This sketch of cultural difference doesn't mean to deprecate American culture, nor to elevate it chauvinistically. The culture is very far from monadic, and it does not have an established place for poetry. We are not Persians or Bengalis. (Though without doubt significant numbers of us are indeed Persian-Americans or Bengali-Americans.) That in those relatively less plural cultures most people quote, recite, and compose poetry as part of a life is attractive, and in each case reflects a particular, long history and the life of a particular language. In that language, certain forms of memory, relatively speaking, are settled and available, in art.

But the eccentricities of Dickinson and Whitman also explore the soul's dependence on memory, and its resistance to memory, though with strangely improvised instruments. Their inventions of form and lexicon reflect a culture where imported, inherited and invented elements jangle or coalesce; where the provinces are in no more clear a relation to any capital than the present is to the past, where the wrestling of curatorship with transformation is palpably strenuous. Underlying that contest, and inspiring invention, is the possibility of a vacuum, of failed memory. Thus, the formal singularities and lacunae of Dickinson and Whitman have served us, in our readerly voices, as the polished, eloquent and overt myth making of *Hiawatha* and *The Midnight Ride of Paul Revere* have not.

A profound, engaging absence is suggested by the terms I have quoted from Tocqueville: "Nothing conceivable is so petty, so insipid, so crowded with paltry interests—in one word, so anti-poetic—as the life of a man in the United States." The eclectic, uneven, improvised life of poetry in the country reflects that absence and a richly characteristic response to it. The Favorite Poem Project undertook to register specific examples of Americans who remembered specific poems. In practice, the undertaking registers the existence of an American readership as intricate, as raw, as original, as many-tongued and as eccentric as the achievements of the great American poets. The goal was less a promotion than a selective, indeed edited, portrait.

VI. Readers

One question such a portrait might illuminate is the place of poetry in relation to a tremendously powerful, elaborate, and often brilliant mass culture. In one way or another, every American poet and reader must respond to that amazing constellation of genius and vulgarity, vitality and turpitude, of which the greatest products are jazz and the American feature film. The decidedly non-statistical, unscientific nature of the project had the advantage, as well as the limitation, of disregarding numbers in favor of instances.

One of the participants we eventually filmed, John Doherty, wrote in his initial correspondence the sentence "I guess a ditchdigger who reads Shakespeare is still just a ditchdigger." And in the video segment, we do in fact see him digging a ditch, wearing his hardhat, wielding a spade as part of his work as a construction worker for the Boston Gas Company. After talking briefly about his work, he reads some passages from Whitman's "Song of Myself." "Poetry," Doherty says in his remarks, "was definitely intimidating at first. It just looked like a lot of words that were out of order and out of place, that did not belong together." He adds, "It takes a lot of reading and re-reading to grasp it."

I believe that in many countries, social constraints of one kind or another might suppress or temper this candor, requiring more automatic respect, greater dissimulation, or less discovery. This freedom to judge the art of poetry itself as a consumer, intimidated by the art's difficulty but not by its social prestige or authority, feels American to me, for good or ill. It is echoed by a number of the participants, including Seph Rodney, who early in his memorable discussion of Sylvia Plath's "Nick and the Candlestick" remarks that he had always thought of poetry as merely "grandiose" and "for want of a better term, a highfalutin . . . not very *real* way of using language." Like Doherty on Whitman, Rodney on Plath presents his attachment to her work as a kind of conversion experience to poetry itself.

Poetry's place in the world and in a particular life seems more self-evident and authoritative for some of the participants who came here from other places, such as Lyn Aye, the Burmese-American anesthesiologist in San Jose, who reads a poem by Zawgee in Burmese and in English translation, or Jayashree Chatterjee, the New Jersey librarian who reads Tagore in Bengali and in English.

What is striking in all four of these instances is a note of personal conviction in both the vocal delivery of the poem each reader selected and in their statements about the poems. The slightly accented Burmese and Indian voices both speak about exile or loss of place, and in what I consider another characteristic American gesture they select poems that simultaneously sharpen and soothe those feelings of homesickness or immigrant dislocation.

In short, the intimacy and introspection of these readers, in their approach to the poems they read, correspond to Tocqueville's proposition about poetry in a democracy. The subject of each poem as they describe it begins with the condition of a soul: material, to borrow Tocqueville's terms, more "vast" for each reader than it is various or "numerous."

Concentration on the individual human soul is audible in the construction worker Doherty's remarkable reading of the closing passage from "Leaves of Grass." The poem's familiar, bizarre mixture of grandiloquence and comedy, egotism and generosity, takes on new overtones as the young man in the video, sitting on an earth-mover, reads the first-person lines:

> The spotted hawk swoops by and accuses me . . . he
>   complains of my gab and my loitering.
>
> I too am not a bit tamed. . . . I too am untranslatable,
> I sound my barbaric yawp over the roofs of the world.
>
> The last scud of day holds back for me,
> It flings my likeness after the rest and true as any on
>   the shadowed wilds.
> It coaxes me to the vapor and the dusk.
>
> I depart as air. . . . I shake my white locks at the
>   runaway sun,
> I effuse my flesh in eddies and drift it in lacy jags.

Whitman's vision of his death and his endurance are read by Doherty as an address to the reader, on a quite pragmatic level. "You will hardly know who I am or what I mean," he reads, and "Failing to fetch me at first keep encouraged, / Missing me one place search another, / I stop somewhere waiting for you." This advice was written, and in this instance was read, in a particular spirit of direct address, an immediacy that means to redefine poetry itself, and makes the vocal, readerly occasion transcendent.

The mass, technological medium of video, perhaps paradoxically, thus dramatizes something I have called crucial about the medium of poetry: Whitman's lines—visibly—taking for their medium John Doherty's breath and hearing as he both enacts and imagines the sounds of the words and sentences. The artificial occasion of the video reminds me that when I read a poem, aloud or not, I am aware of it as something to say, or that could be said. The vehicle for that awareness is in my bodily senses—a vehicle, also, for memory as when I chant the phone number or the grocery list, manifesting some evolutionary link between vocal rhythm and recalled information.

The reader is not merely the performer of the poem, but an actual, living medium for the poem. Though viewers may feel that Doherty reads the lines well, it is the embodiment of the poem, not his or any performance, that is essential. The poem takes place in each reader, more fundamentally than on any screen or stage. In relation to mass media, this distinction seems to me crucial: if the medium is, above all, any one reader's voice, or any one reader's ears, then the art is by its nature, inherently, on an individual and personal scale.

In its intimacy and human presence, reading a poem may resemble a live performance, as distinct from a mass-produced image such as a movie (or, indeed, a video of someone reciting a poem). Insofar as its text is fixed, the poem, like a play in this respect, is distinctly less ephemeral than the live performance.

Poetry's dual qualities of human scale and permanence are roughly parallel to the dread of homogenizing uniformity on one side and the fragmented, violently solipsistic life of the Cyclopes, who have no mores or community, on the other side. Poetry's voice—its literal, actual voice—takes on a heightened poignancy, and a heightened value, in a culture rich in dazzling performative art that is produced, duplicated and marketed on a mass scale.

Spectacle, too, is not the point. A principle in making the videos was never to illustrate the poem: no footage of a snow man for Wallace Stevens's "The Snow Man." In the setting of mass culture, the voice of poetry, in ways that entertainment media cannot, embodies something crucially different from spectacle: an intense concentration on individual consciousness.

To put this another way, the videos reveal that one can see a person read a poem. I can watch your face while you listen to music, watch a movie, or look at visual art—but I am not witnessing your experience of that work. The same goes for watching a reader deep in a novel. To watch someone saying a poem aloud can be to witness that person's experience of the poem. The readers in the videos, though they know that they are being filmed, make visible the intimate and singular penetration of the art. Their "performances" of the poems are not artistic performances. The reader's voice is different from actorly interpretations of the poem's emotions and ideas—though those are surely present—but something subtly different from that: presentations of what it is like when Seph Rodney or Lynn Aye or John Doherty reads a particular poem.

Tocqueville's speculations about equality on one hand, and on the other contemporary mass culture with its emphasis on performance, on lavish spectacle and reproduction, combine to make me hear with special urgency the particular reader's voice: its regional accent, its sense of an individual life, and its relation to the cadences and meanings of the words, as it utters:

> You will hardly know who I am or what I mean,
> But I shall be good health to you nevertheless,
> And filter and fiber your blood.

VII. The Narcissistic
and the Personal

When the Favorite Poem Project has been described approvingly as "populist" I have felt uncomfortable, because I know that the approach was in essential ways elitist. There is a generation that loves the writing of Robert Service, and some of them wrote cogent letters in response to the project, and some of their grandchildren wrote about Shel Silverstein. Some from the generations between those two wrote to us about Rod McKuen, or the lyrics of Bob Dylan—all part of the larger archive of letters and e-mails, and significant elements in that archive, but not represented in the book or the recordings, by fiat of us editors.

On the other hand, we were guided by respect for the ways nonprofessional readers read and the ways they describe their reading. This element of the project has excited some negative judgment. Pov Chin, a teenager from California who is represented both in the anthology and in the videos, wrote:

My interpretation of this poem written by Langston Hughes may not be the same as his. But a poem is what I choose to make of it and this one is a description of me. It explains how I feel about life.

A reviewer took this statement as his leading example of a defect he found in the book. After quoting these sentences, he writes:

> This theme—*this is a description of me*—occurs again and again. . . . Rather than letting poems draw us out of ourselves, making us larger and broader, we are encouraged to make the poems smaller so that we can take them inside us and, in a literal sense, comprehend them. . . . Pinsky and Dietz may simply have assumed that the only way to sell poetry to Americans is to appeal to their inherent narcissism.*

In its way, this makes a certain sense. (The reviewer, incidentally, quotes Tocqueville about American pettiness and self-centeredness, but not about the "more vast" subjects for poetry.) The terms of the Favorite Poem invitation did invite the volunteers to say something about their particular, personal reasons for selecting the poem. Indeed, when putting together the anthology and the recordings, an explicit criterion for selection was the intensity and interest of what the reader had to say about the poem. It could be argued that this editorial inclination vulgarized the project, or at least distorted it toward the personal or introspective, and away from the poem as a means of discovery about the world, or as a highly developed work of art.

* Troy Jollimore, *Boston Book Review*, March 2000.

But the cliche of American narcissism does not adequately describe what these people actually say. Let me return to the example of Pov Chin, who says, "this poem is a description of me." Her voice and accent in the video are those of a California teenager, and this prefatory statement of hers (partly a statement, in my understanding of it, of diffidence) can sound glib or self-centered. The poem is an extremely short one by Langston Hughes, far from his most impressive work:

Minstrel Man

Because my mouth
Is wide with laughter
And my throat
Is deep with song,
You do not think
I suffer after
I have held my pain
So long?
Because my mouth
Is wide with laughter,
You do not hear
My inner cry?
Because my feet
Are gay with dancing,
You do not know
I die?

The little paradigm of this poem, as plain as a folk song, takes on rich overtones and vibrations in relation to the American minstrel tradition of blackface—makeup that was sometimes worn by black, as well as white, performers. The grinning minstrel-show performer, bursting with joy, represents a terrible and complicated process of cultural appropriation and distortion, all sorts of sublimated guilts and envies and myths, comforting and disturbing.

Of all that, the young student Pov Chin appears to have been unaware. When she found the poem and copied it out, she tells us, she had not heard of Langston Hughes. It is not clear if she knew at the time that he was African-American, or what the information signifies to her, particularly since she was born in Laos of Cambodian parents. Yet what she says about the poem is historically germane, and perhaps increases one's esteem for Hughes's poem. In the book, she writes:

> I am not free. I am a female Cambodian growing up in America but I am raised in the old-fashioned Cambodian ways. Asian tradition for daughters is very strict. It is so hard for me to see my friends having a sleep-over and the only person missing is me. I walk around school with a big smile on my face but inside I am a caged bird just waiting to be free. Life has never been easy for me especially with my parents' problems. Their problems started during the Khmer Rouge genocide in the early '70s. Two of their sons passed away in front of their faces, killed by the Khmer Rouge. They still had the courage to get out of Cambodia and find refuge for us in America.

This is not literary criticism, nor does it pretend to be. But the word for it is not "narcissism," either, and as an explanation of why the writer values "Minstrel Man" by Langston Hughes, it is forceful and appropriate. The association of freedom and cultural restraint with performance, the equation of "big smile" with being caged, represent an insightful tribute to Hughes's poem. To the extent that Pov Chin didn't know much about the author, it is remarkably intuitive. Even the exclusion from the American high-school custom of sleep-overs and the delicate euphemism "passed away" for the murdered children testify to a rich and respectful relation to the poem.

The distinction between the narcissistic and the personal, abundantly clear in this letter quoted in the anthology, is even more clear in the video segment artfully filmed by Emiko Omori. In the opening shot Pov Chin begins speaking in the foreground; in the background, behind her, we see a suburban-looking interior and first a television set playing something with Asian faces and language and then, as the camera pans upward, the seated figure of a woman. This watchful figure, present throughout the shot, is clearly Pov Chin's mother, silently following the interview as though she is not willing to let this, one of her remaining children, out of her sight. We see a shrine, and some incense being lit and some family photographs: of children posing in front of a modest house; of an unsmiling elderly woman.

A notable aspect of Pov Chin's narration comes with her explanation that during the family ordeal and the murder of the little boys she was not yet born; the mother was pregnant. "It was not only us," she says, "it was my granny, too, and they killed my granny." The first person plural of "only us" is striking: "they rounded us up" she says at another point. This unselfconscious first-person plural, like the watching maternal figure, embodies the powerful familial and social component of the sentences quoted in the anthology, and echoes similar questions of the generic and the individual, inside and outside, cultural cage and cultural sustenance, in Hughes's poem. The first-person singular of "I am not free" is related to the first-person plural of "they rounded us up"; both sentences acknowledge the great conundrum of each person's connection to others. Whatever one understands that "we" to represent, it is not narcissism.

I have quoted a somewhat negative response to the project (and the review I've quoted from is in fact only partly negative) less to contradict it than to suggest the range of cultural and literary responses that this undertaking has called up, partly by accident. Questions about an anthology, or about what is narcissistic, what is personal, are ripples in a great flood of ambiguities and agitations. My proposition is that the reviewer's gesture against a leveling uniformity and the Favorite Poem Project's gesture toward a unifying cultural ground, though they seem like opposite actions, both express a somewhat anxious defense—or pursuit—of shared memory.

VIII. Models of Culture

A successful, inventive mass culture, together with Tocqueville's "principle of equality" from which the mass culture partly grows, have engendered a need to define, and perhaps to construct, the social place of an ancient art. This pressure should not be seen as merely negative; it, too, is enabling as well as controlling. The mass culture itself struggles to adjust memory and change, and like the poets it sometimes succeeds and sometimes collapses into pretension or banality. In the absence of the settled aristocratic idea, and in the absence of the unifying folk culture, Americans have been pressed to supply new forms of memory.

Responding to this pressure, Whitman became brokenhearted by his inability to create (and fill) the role of national bard. That sadness was re-enforced for me by my own rather naive surprise at how journalists responded to President Clinton's gift of *Leaves of Grass* to Monica Lewinsky: they apparently thought of Whitman not as the quintessential American poet, but as the author of a rather hot book.

Nonetheless, the vacuum or pressure that created and frustrated Whitman's ambitions also inspired his mighty and mightily driven achievement. And the unsettled place of poetry has continued to inspire great works as well as blather and despair: the poetry of both William Carlos Williams and Wallace Stevens, for example, can be seen as growing more or less explicitly out of the question of poetry's place in national manners. "The spirit and space," writes Stevens in his poem "The American Sublime": "The empty spirit / In vacant space. / What wine does one drink? / What bread does one eat?" To take a less sublime example, improvising the figurative bread, the wine, the place, Americans have invented MFA degrees, poetry slams, coffee houses, small press cooperatives: sometimes gawky, yet sometimes vital or excellent cultural structures. The audio recordings, videos and anthology of the Favorite Poem Project are one more gesture of this kind of improvisation, and in some measure give an account of that improvisation, as well.

I'm afraid that to make my point I may have exaggerated the uniqueness of the United States. All culture, after all, like any living person's memory, perpetually adds and rearranges, drops and inflects its material: culture is a process of change and adaptation, not a static entity or a list of works. The more I knew about Iran and India, the more, I am sure, I would have to modify my assumptions about Persian and Bengali poetry, and their readership as I imagine it, talking through my hat—the more flux and ambiguity I would perceive.

Still, American culture as I have experienced it seems so much in process, so brilliantly and sometimes brutally in motion, that standard models for it fail to apply. The Mandarin notion of a privileged elite preserving cultural goods on an old-world model is swamped by the demotic genius of characteristic makers like Herman Melville, Emily Dickinson, Preston Sturges, Duke Ellington, William Carlos Williams. The Arnoldian model of cultural missionaries' bringing along the masses wilts not only for the same reason but because modern political history has discredited the notion that intellectual or artistic figures can, automatically or by their nature, serve as moral leaders. The Mandarin's complementary opposite, the Philistine model, would accept the marketplace entirely: whatever is consumed is good. This idea collapses before the omnivorous, strangely vaunting aspiration of actual Americans—with the Favorite Poem Project one current source of examples. Another model, the idea of mass culture as our only real culture, cannot do because culture is a process of memory, and as mass cultural products speed by, the popular culture of each decade is winnowed to be preserved in the care of universities, libraries, foundations. A serious task of criticism is to assist in that winnowing process. In the archives of curatorship, classic jazz and silent comedy and blues await any of the best of our sitcoms or rap performers that deserve remembering.

And the model of American culture as a mere confederation of ethnic or regional or religious or gender-based cultures cannot suffice. Our greatest achievements—a poem by Dickinson or a chorus by Parker—are as mixed, syncretic and eclectic as our inventions in food or clothing. In that polyglot, heuristic and erratic flux, each of the non-professional readers included in the recordings, anchored by the vocal attachment to a poem, offers a reference point: the impurity and idiosyncracy of a cultural fact.

The culture has no model as a fixed state or a curriculum: it is a process, characterized by unanticipated shifts and improvisations. Nor is it necessary to sentimentalize that process. Triviality and pedantry, bigotry and complacency—these aspects of the larger culture, too, could be reflected by the microcosm of the letters received by the Favorite Poem Project, if that were its goal. Poetry is not the voice of virtue and right thinking—not the rhyme department of any progressive movement. It is a commonplace that great poets have espoused repulsive politics. The turns of verse, between justified and ragged, the regular and the unique, the spoken and the implied, the private and the social, profoundly embody not a moral, but a cultural quest for life between a barren isolation on one side and an enveloping mass on the other. That quest is the action of poetry's voice.

IX. Conclusion

I will quote one of my own favorite poems—one I have written about before, in an account of my home town on the Jersey Shore. Written near the beginning of the twentieth century by Edwin Arlington Robinson, "Eros Turannos" epitomizes for me the tidal forces within lyric poetry that draw it toward social reality. The poem's peculiar, rather spectacular form embodies those forces and their "War," as Bishop calls it, with something private and interior. In its title and other echoes of Greek tragedy, in its focus on one heroic figure in her choral, provincial setting, "Eros Turannos" recalls the individual's cultural anxieties of suffocation on one side and an isolating dearth on the other.

The protagonist is a woman who must choose between a love affair that she well knows will be a calamity, or no love affair at all. The extraordinary account of her psychology turns out, partway through the poem, to be voiced by a town, in the first person plural:

Eros Turannos

She fears him, and will always ask
   What fated her to choose him;
She meets in his engaging mask
   All reasons to refuse him;
But what she meets and what she fears
Are less than are the downward years
Drawn slowly to the foamless weirs
   Of age, were she to lose him.

Between a blurred sagacity
   That once had power to sound him,
And Love, that will not let him be
   The Judas that she found him,
Her pride assuages her almost,
As if it were alone the cost.
He sees that he will not be lost,
   And waits and looks around him.

A sense of ocean and old trees
   Envelops and allures him;
Tradition, touching all he sees,
   Beguiles and reassures him;
And all her doubts of what he says
Are dimmed with what she knows of days—
Till even prejudice delays,
   And fades, and she secures him.

The falling leaf inaugurates
   The reign of her confusion;

The pounding wave reverberates
   The dirge of her illusion;
And home, where passion lived and died,
Becomes a place where she can hide,
While all the town and harbor side
   Vibrate with her seclusion.

We tell you, tapping on our brows,
   The story as it should be,
As if the story of a house
   Were told, or ever could be;
We'll have no kindly veil between
Her visions and those we have seen,
As if we guessed what hers have been,
   Or what they are or would be.

Meanwhile we do no harm; for they
   That with a god have striven,
Not hearing much of what we say,
   Take what the god has given;
Though like waves breaking it may be,
Or like a changed familiar tree,
Or like a stairway to the sea
   Where down the blind are driven.

The astoundingly deployed rhymes make "Eros Turannos" a
kind of hyper-ballad: a ballad to the ballad power, as though the
woman's isolation and shame call up some longing for a folk-
tradition that her surroundings cannot provide. On this level,
Thompson's idea that the cadences of verse imitate the shape of
sentences has a kind of palpable application. More explicitly,

the first person plural as "we" tap our brows and tell the story impersonates the communal, but also heightens the central character's loneliness and lack.

That lack is made more poignant for me by what I know of Robinson's career. For the long first part of it, he was indigent, lonely, spurned by magazine editors, embittered with his provincial town in Maine and with the New York where he also found the going hard.

But on the other hand, the town does notice the woman's fate, and registers it and recounts it with awe. On this subject, let me quote the letter about this poem quoted in *Americans' Favorite Poems*—the only letter in the anthology that we editors print anonymously:

> I discovered the poem many years ago as a newly married girl living in a small town, which in fact possesses a harborside. My husband had an intractable (it seemed then) drug and alcohol problem and was away a lot for his job. I didn't have a job at the time, knew no one, and spent many days in solitude riding my bike, reading, and reflecting on what my life had become since my decision to marry. I did not then comprehend what the line "for they that with a god have striven" meant. I just recognized completely the state of wishing to be united with a man because of what I knew or thought I knew about the onward years. I lived then and now in an ancient house left me by my father, whose father left it to him, whose father left it to him. It is one mile from the ocean, surrounded by old trees. These facts made up no small part of my husband's decision to marry me. I copied that poem into the

journal I kept then and it sits before me on the table as I write. I have always felt the woman was as I was. The knowledge that I've gained about "the god" has lent a retrospective dignity to events experienced as utter failure. The discovery of the poem, with its eerily large number of coincidences with my own situation, was like a gift, or maybe a clue in a giant game of charades, from "the god" himself, who saw he had perhaps misjudged his opponent.

This personal account of the poem is as remarkable as the coincidences it notes. Its viewpoint is perhaps more psychological and social than literary. The writer, for all her power and eloquence, does not choose to consider the ways that the poem's story may be Robinson's story, a transformed account of his own frustration, loneliness, dignity and rage. But this insightful, anonymous letter also suggests something like the classical relation of tragic hero and community, or touches on that idea with the words "a retrospective dignity." In the poem, the community gains a certain stature from its awareness that in it is one who has wrestled with a god; the individual gains dignity from the witnessing of that struggle. The man, who "waits and looks around him," is in a significant way less important than the god or the town. The poem is less about two people than it is about one person, who deals with love as a ruling force, and with a social setting.

The form of poetry in "Eros Turannos," the chiming and symmetrically swirling rhymes, give rich voice to a great solitude, a desolation that communicates itself to the very landscape. "A sense of ocean and old trees" is vague partly as a mocking evocation of the man who looks around him, lightly comic in a way like the "iron clothing" of Robinson's nostalgist Miniver Cheevy. But the phrase also has a specificity that relates it to Robinson's concluding image, the "stairway to the sea / Where down the blind are driven." The nightmare ritual or flight suggested by that image calls up a social world more ancient or more fantastically barbarian than can be known. The voice of the poem, in our heads and in our breath, brings that archaic world and the solitude of the protagonist together, with terror and majesty.

"Eros Turannos" was published in the same issue of *Poetry* magazine as Carl Sandburg's group of *Chicago Poems*, including "Chicago"—the well-known anthology piece (it appears in the Favorite Poem anthology), the prolonged apostrophe that begins "Hog Butcher for the World" and ends "Freight Handler to the Nation." "Chicago" is not a bad piece of writing, despite the limitations I have indicated with the phrase "anthology piece." In no way does it begin to equal "Eros Turannos" in emotion, in formal penetration or invention.

But Sandburg's group was made the leading item in that issue of *Poetry*, and that year received the magazine's Levinson Prize, which Yvor Winters in his book on Robinson says was "the most considerable prize offered for poetry in the United States at that time."* With the arrogance of the living, we may deceive ourselves that nowadays we know better. What's germane here is the way these two poems approach their subjects, and their implied subject of how poetry will situate itself in relation to American life.

It may be that the judges admired the vitality of Sandburg's epithets and participles: "Laughing the stormy, husky, brawling

* Winters, *Edwin Arlington Robinson* (New York: Norton, 1971), p. 11.

laughter of Youth, half-naked, sweating, proud to be Hog Butcher. . . ." Indeed, they may have found his poem engaging and engaged precisely in relation to my subject in these lectures: poetry's voice in American culture. Where "Eros Turannos" might have seemed laudable but modest in scope—a character study or an anecdote—Sandburg's dithyrambic embrace of Chicago as "laughing with white teeth" may have seemed not only original but *avant-garde*.

Comparison of the two poems helps define a place for American poetry, its profound role of both engaging and resisting the rather Sandburgesque giant of a society that is at once dazzling and banal, provincial and global, menacing and hopeful. Poetry's voice participates in that society and its culture, but by its nature also resists them: singular where they are plural, memory-driven where they are heedless, personal where they are impersonal—luxuriously slow where they are rushed, and thrillingly swift where they are plodding.

I speak as an enthusiast of modern life: I enjoy the possibilities of jet travel, the DVD and the VCR, am devoted to my computer and my cell phone, appreciate the marvels of contemporary plumbing, medicine, dentistry. Like Frank Bidart in his recent poem "For the Twentieth Century," I am grateful for the technologies that make Callas, Laurel & Hardy, Szigeti available at a touch of the PLAY button, turning their art into "pattern, form / whose infinite // repeatability within matter / defies matter." But the voice that appreciates the artists and the "thousand / technologies of ecstasy" that preserve them is also idiosyncratic, not duplicable, and resistantly inward as well as outward.

What Robinson resisted in 1911 was a provincial vacuum, the nightmare of us small-town watchers who can gossip and tap our brows but cannot make tragedies or ballads. A village stinginess haunts his work and this poem in particular, recalling Tocqueville's description of American life: "so petty, so insipid, so crowded with paltry interests." There is something heroic in Robinson's simultaneous resistant loathing and meticulous love for the provincial settings and figures he imagined, the lonely grandeur of his hypertrophied ballad stanzas and saturated ironies. Devising a courtly telling for the materials of barren gossip, Robinson suggests the rich enigmas and promises of the American setting. Sandburg has considerable merits, but by comparison his poem's rebellions are trivial, and its celebrations coarse.

"Chicago" responds to the dread of sectarian dissolution, of a culture too weak to hold together, by constructing a brilliant but rather bullying journalistic rhetoric that is covertly general, for all its apparent specificity: there is no specter of isolation in his poem because he does not include even the possibility of loneliness. In another direction, "Chicago" deals with anxiety about an enveloping, centralized mass culture with expert, infectious pep-talk: what Sandburg's poem resists, ultimately, is discouragement. As an ostensible "barbaric yawp" it is studied and domesticated.

Robinson, like the hero of his poem, wrestled with something larger than himself, and like hers his wrestling deserves a grave and enthralled communal awe. His peculiar blend of ballad and tragedy, meditation and gossip, resists the cultural stereotypes and the literary clichés of his own time and of ours.

His command of specificity and abstraction, his managing of idiom and lines, resist in an anticipatory way any invitation to make American poetry something that goes down easily: a part of show business, or a branch of literary theory, or any other diminished thing.

"Eros Turannos" is arresting and spectacular, in the chamber of spirit and ear that I have suggested is the place of poetry. It answers and evokes our anxieties about mass culture with an individual, enigmatic fate. It answers and evokes our anxieties about fragmentation with the fiery ingenuity of its cadences, the audacity of its references. To the American thesis of a deadening absence of culture and its antithesis, a devouring omni-culture, the poem responds with a synthesis that includes both a provincial tapping of our brows and the image of the blind driven down a stairway to the sea—all in the single breath of the poet's invention. Robinson's homely word "house" makes the fate-driven family of Atreus simultaneous with the pilasters and spandrels of a seaside village manse.

These are the inclusions and audacities of American art: not tamed by expectation, untranslatable by journalism or pedantry, outlandish, even barbaric, sounding its yawps somewhere over our worldly roofs, or beyond them.

INDEX OF NAMES

A NOTE ON THE TYPE

This book has been composed in Arno, an Old-style serif typeface in the classic Venetian tradition, designed by Robert Slimbach at Adobe.

GPSR Authorized Representative: Easy Access System Europe - Mustamäe tee 50, 10621 Tallinn, Estonia, gpsr.requests@easproject.com

www.ingramcontent.com/pod-product-compliance
Lightning Source LLC
Chambersburg PA
CBHW011643010726
47495CB00011B/2879